3-D ART PROJECTS
THAT TEACH

by
Lynn Brisson

Incentive Publications, Inc.
Nashville, TN

Illustrated by Lynn Brisson
Cover by Susan Eaddy
Edited by Sally Sharpe

ISBN 0-86530-084-4

TABLE OF CONTENTS

Preface 7

Feathered Friends 9

Open House Invitation 12

Charlie The Clown 14

Molly Mouse And The Months Of The Year 19

Polite Penguins 22

Friendly Freddy Frog 25

Robbie Robot 28

The Little Learning Engine 31

Bubbles The Goldfish 34

Katie The Kangaroo 36

Turtle Town 39

Wordy Worm 46

Clever Chicken 48

From Seed To Plant 50

I Wonder What's Under The Sea 53

Dinosaurs 56

Paper Pals 61

Pop-up Ghost 66

Terrific Turkey 68

Lollipop Ornaments 70

Bountiful Baskets 71

Happy Tooth 77

PREFACE

This book contains out-of-the-ordinary art activities designed to provide young students with enjoyable art experiences as well as to teach basic skills. You will be able to "cross the curriculum" as students engage in unique art projects and use the finished products to reinforce skills in math, reading, and other subject areas!

All of the projects in this book are three-dimensional or have manipulative parts. Materials listings, easy-to-follow instructions, and actual-size patterns make the projects quick and easy to create and fun to use. By using a simple cut and fold technique, students will be able to turn "ordinary" patterns into exciting 3-D creations — all by themselves!

Suggestions for use are included with each activity to give you creative ideas for using the projects. For example, a 3-D frog can be used for "leap frog" math games and a lily pad display as well as for name or place cards. The activities are perfect for decorating classrooms and bulletin boards, for making invitations and 3-D notes, and for creating special "take home" projects. You'll find many other ways to use these fun activities to suit your own classroom and student needs!

FEATHERED FRIENDS

MATERIALS:
- construction paper
- crayons or markers
- glue
- scissors

CONSTRUCTION:
1. Reproduce and cut out the patterns.
2. Cut the patterns out of construction paper and/or color the patterns with crayons or markers.
3. Glue the bird patterns together as instructed on the pattern page.
4. Glue the bird and leaves to the branch.
5. Glue the bird and birdhouse on a sheet of construction paper.

USE:
- Create a "welcome back to school" bulletin board display. Ask the students to omit step 5 and to write their names on the branches. The students may attach their birds and branches to the bulletin board.
- Have the students complete this 3-D activity as part of a unit on birds or as a celebration of spring.

Leaves

Branch

cut along dotted lines

fold over & glue

fold over & glue

glue 2 bird patterns together

Bird Patterns

10

Birdhouse

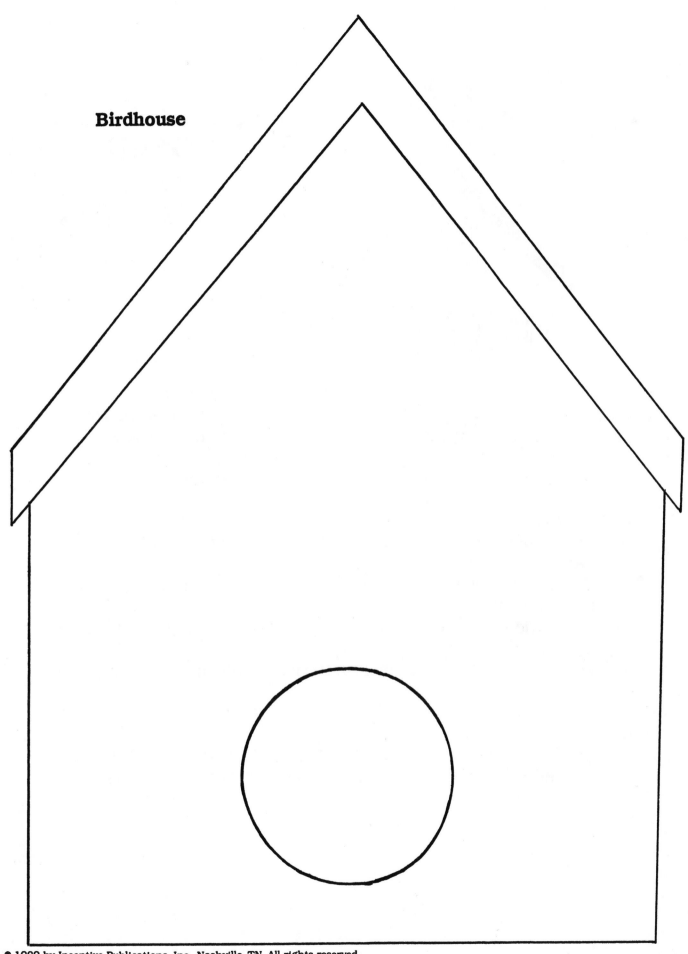

MATERIALS:
- construction paper
- crayons or markers
- glue
- scissors

CONSTRUCTION:
1. Reproduce and cut out the schoolhouse and schoolhouse door patterns.
2. Cut the patterns out of construction paper and/or color the patterns with crayons or markers.
3. Write the date and time of the open house on the inside of the schoolhouse door.
4. Fold the schoolhouse door pattern in half and glue it to the schoolhouse.

USE:
- Students will enjoy helping to make invitations for the school's open house. Send the invitations home with the students.

Schoolhouse door

Schoolhouse

Date: Oct. 3
Time: 7:00

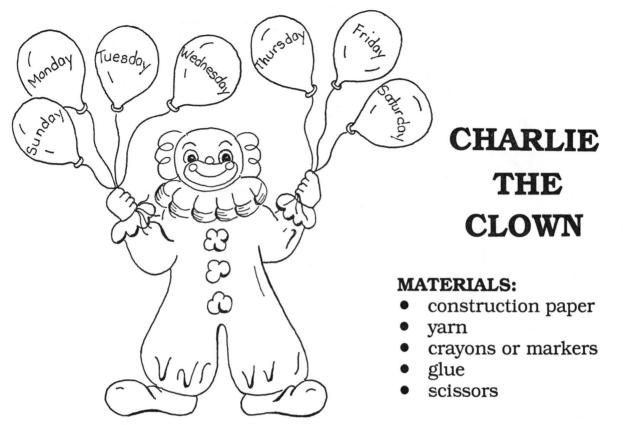

CHARLIE THE CLOWN

MATERIALS:
- construction paper
- yarn
- crayons or markers
- glue
- scissors

CONSTRUCTION:
1. Reproduce and cut out the patterns.
2. Cut the patterns out of construction paper and/or color the patterns with crayons or markers.
3. Make 3-D balloons by following the instructions on the pattern page and glue strings of yarn to the backs of the balloons.
4. Glue the clown patterns together and attach the balloons to the clown's hands.
5. Glue the circus tent top to a piece of construction paper to make a circus tent.

USE:
- Assemble the patterns to make a bulletin board display:
  - Let the students make 3-D balloons for the board. Have the students write their names on the balloons. Use the caption "Our class is fun!"
  - Use the bulletin board to teach different subjects such as days of the week, number concepts, the alphabet, colors, math, etc. (refer to the following page).
- Use Charlie the clown as a wall display. Write special messages on the balloons to announce birthdays, good behavior, etc.

3-D Balloon

cut along dotted lines

fold over
& glue

fold over
& glue

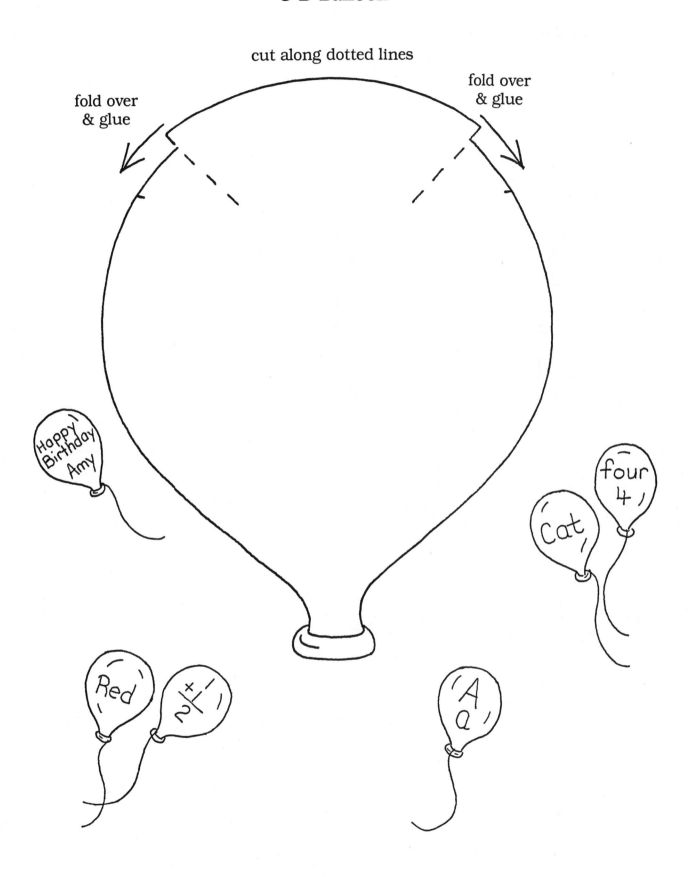

Charlie the Clown (I)

Charlie the Clown (II)

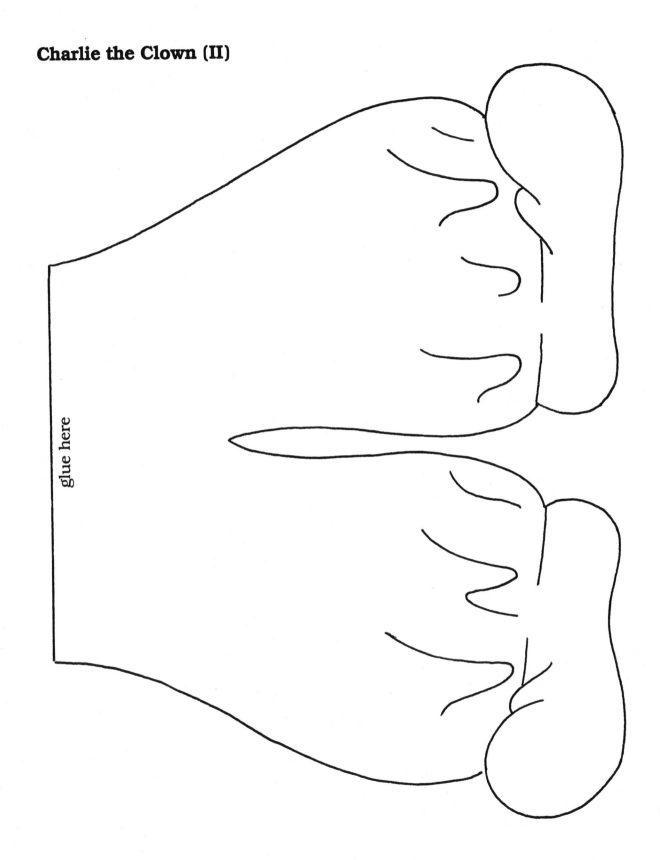

glue here

Circus Tent Top

MOLLY MOUSE AND THE MONTHS OF THE YEAR

MATERIALS:

- construction paper
- crayons or markers
- tissue paper rolls
- pipe cleaners
- stapler
- glue
- scissors

CONSTRUCTION:

1. Reproduce and cut out the patterns.
2. Cut the patterns out of construction paper and/or color the patterns with crayons or markers.
3. Write the months of the year in the cheese holes.
4. Assemble a bulletin board as shown above. Have the students make 3-D mice for the board by following these directions:
   - Cut the top 1/3 off of a tissue paper roll.
   - Staple this section to the center of the tissue paper roll.
   - Use markers and construction paper to add eyes, ears, whiskers, and other features.
   - Add a pipe cleaner tail.

   ### USE:
   - Use the bulletin board display to teach other subjects by writing information in the cheese holes.
   - Group the 3-D mice and a "blank" cheese on a bulletin board. Use the caption "Our work is really cheesy!" Roll up students' papers and stuff them in the mice for display!
   - Let the students make 3-D mice to use as pencil holders (the pipe cleaner tails help the mice stand upright!).

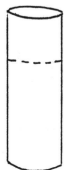
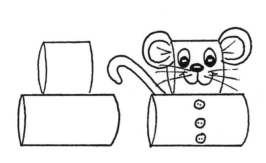
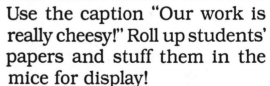

Tail

glue here

Molly Mouse

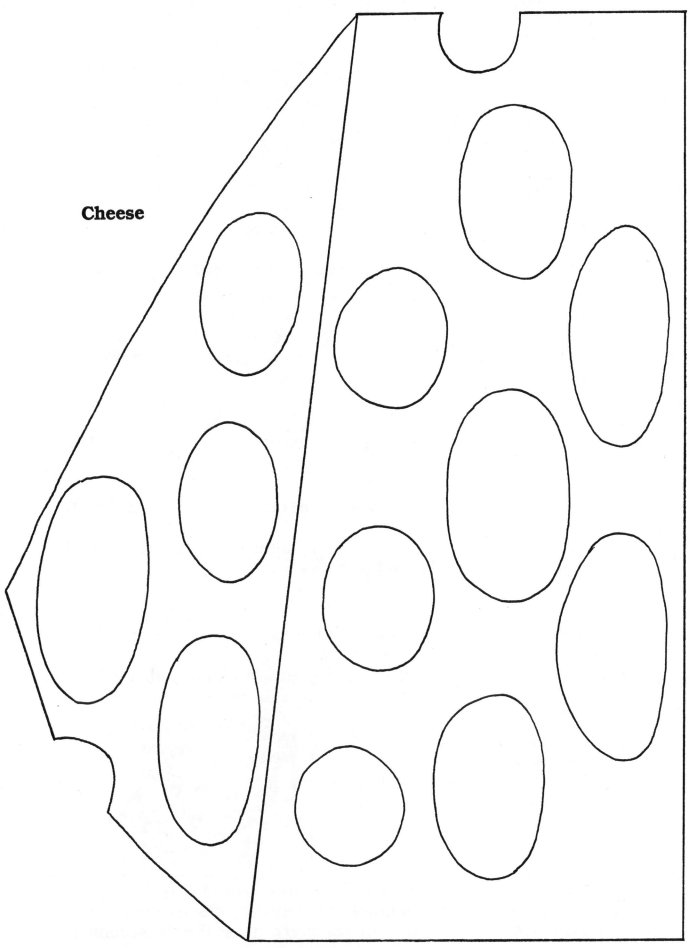

Cheese

POLITE PENGUINS

MATERIALS:
* construction paper
* crayons or markers
* glue
* scissors

CONSTRUCTION:
1. Reproduce and cut out the patterns.
2. Cut the patterns out of construction paper and/or color them with crayons or markers.
3. Glue the eyes and beak on the penguin's head.
4. Cut, fold and glue the penguin II pattern as directed on the pattern page and glue it to the penguin I pattern.
5. Glue two feet to the penguin.
6. Write a classroom "good behavior" rule on a sign and glue the sign to the penguin.
7. Display several 3-D penguins with signs on a bulletin board having the caption "Polite Penguins."

USE:
* Construct the bulletin board display at the first of the year to establish good classroom behavior.
* Substitute different captions and signs to teach and reinforce other subjects and topics.
    * safety rules
    * cafeteria behavior
    * good health habits
    * grammar and punctuation rules
    * vocabulary words
    * etc.
* Ask each student to make a 3-D penguin and to write his or her name and three unique hobbies, interests, or personality traits on a sign. Display the penguins on the wall outside the classroom for a penguin parade!

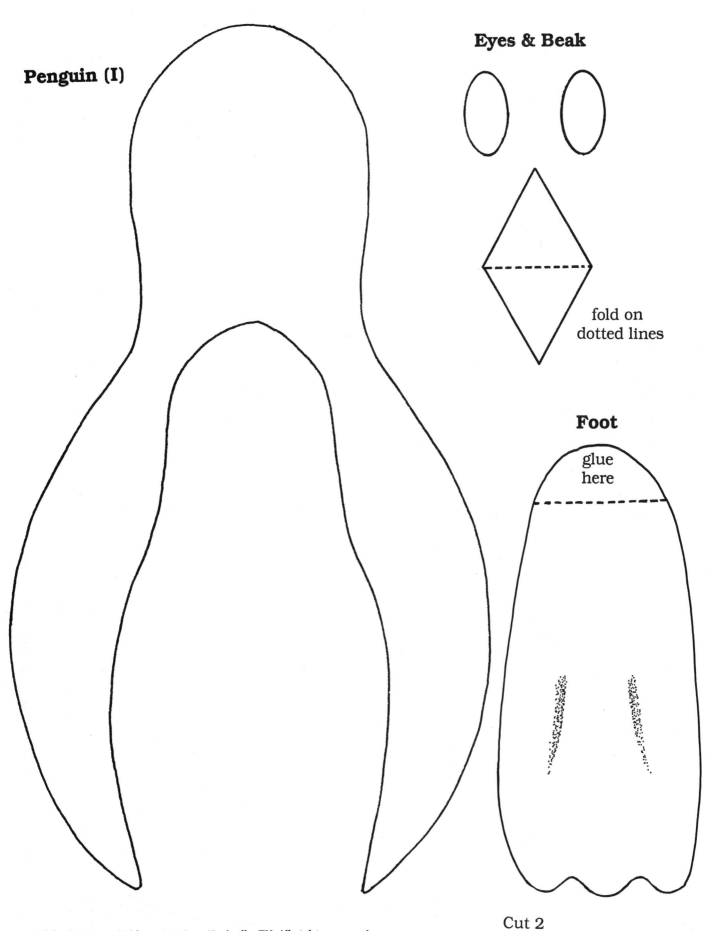

Penguin (I)

Eyes & Beak

fold on
dotted lines

Foot

glue
here

Cut 2

23

Sign

Penguin (II)

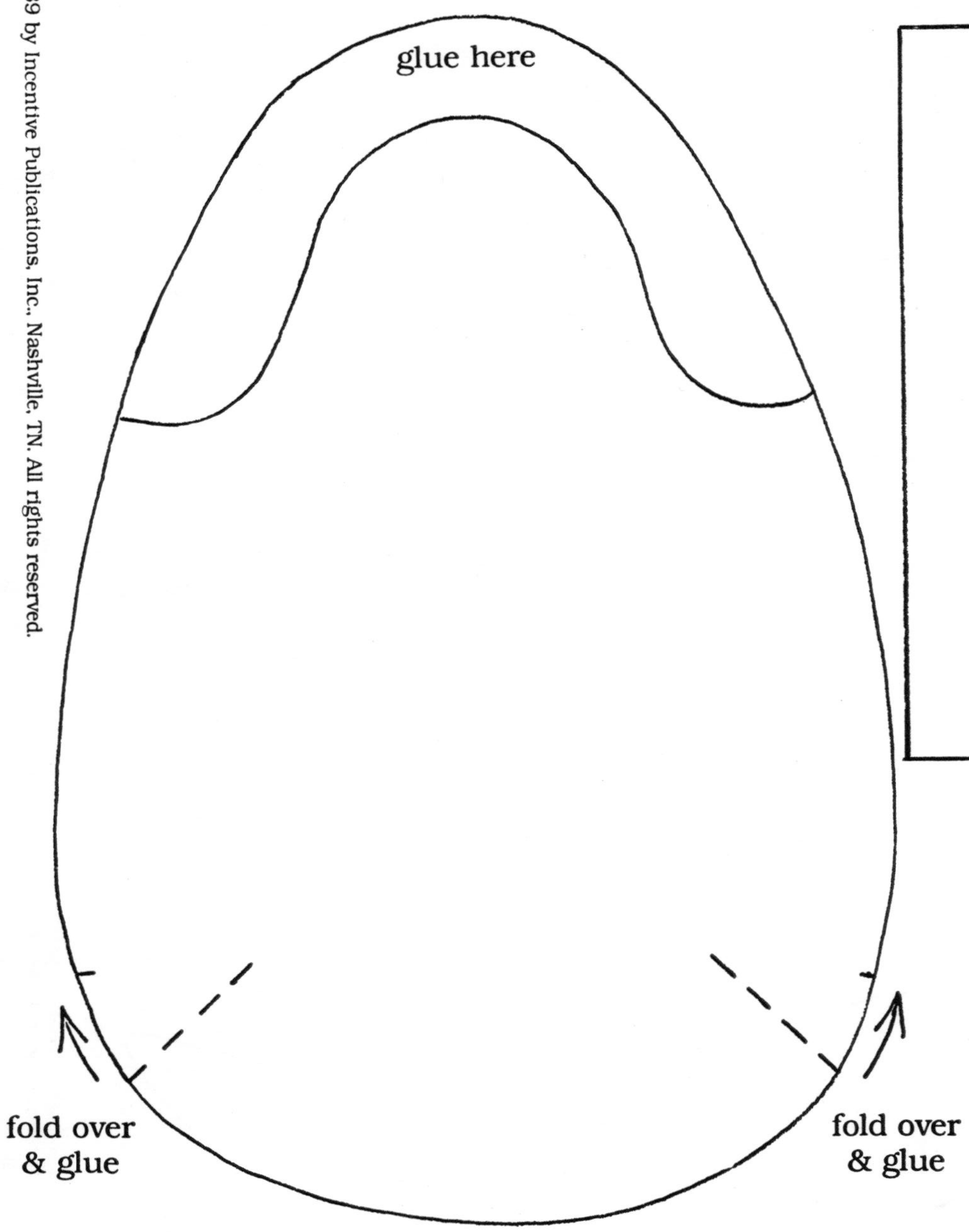

glue here

fold over & glue

cut along dotted lines

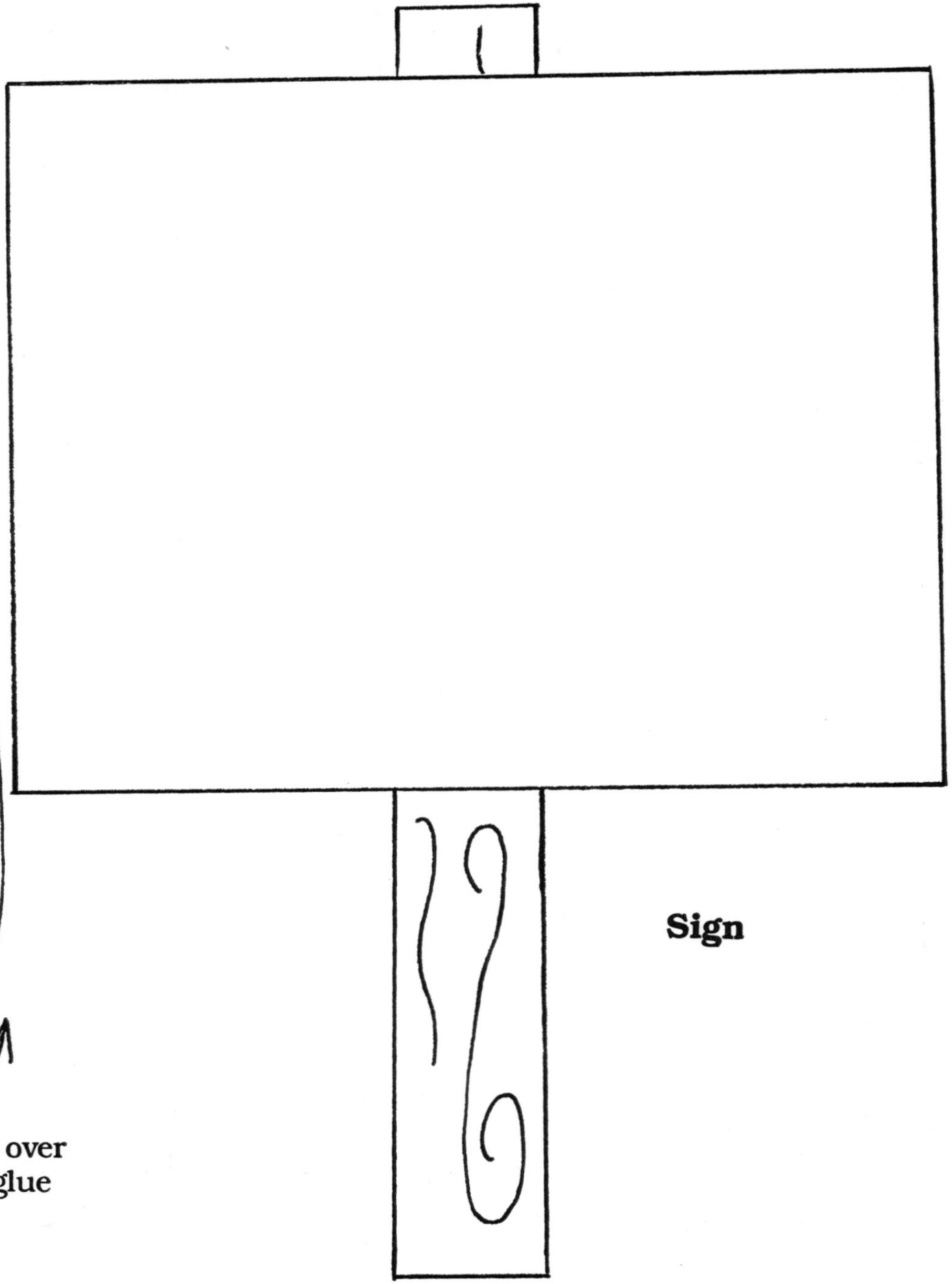

fold over & glue

FRIENDLY FREDDY FROG

Lily Pad Pond

MATERIALS:
- construction paper
- crayons or markers
- glue
- scissors

CONSTRUCTION:
1. Reproduce and cut out the patterns.
2. Cut the patterns out of construction paper and/or color the patterns with crayons or markers.
3. Cut, fold, and glue the frog II pattern as instructed on the pattern page and glue it to the frog I pattern. Bend the body just a little to make the frog stand up.
4. Fold under the flower tab and glue it to the lily pad.
5. Place the frog on the lily pad.

USE:
- Make a lily pad pond display. Cut a "pond" out of blue construction paper and place it on a table. Have each student make a 3-D frog and lily pad to place in the pond.
- Use the frogs to reinforce math concepts. Write a numeral on each frog and the operation sign for addition, subtraction, multiplication and division on four frogs. Let the students "jump" the frogs and signs to play "leap frog" math.
- Use the frogs and lily pads as name cards! Write each student's name on a frog and place the frogs and lily pads on the students' desks or on a working table to mark each student's work area (great for open house!).

Frog (I)

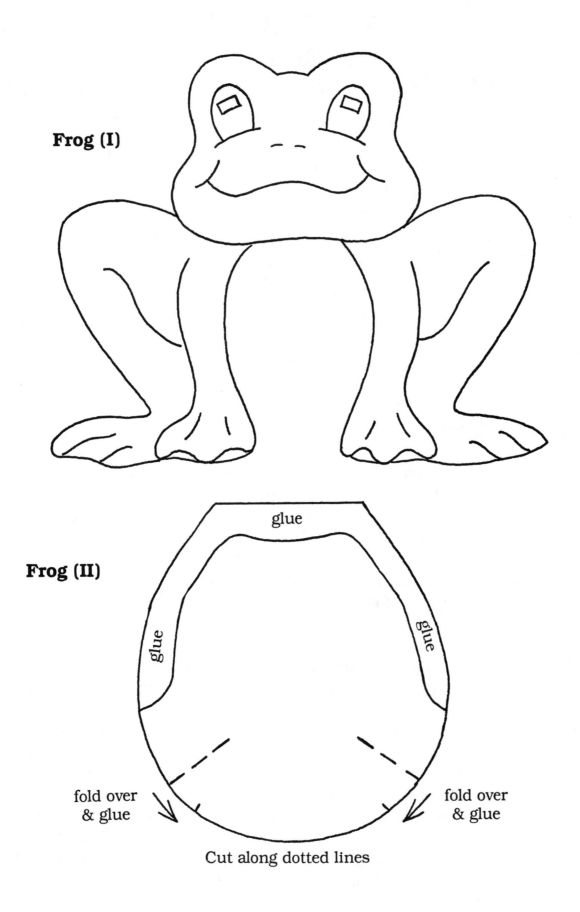

Frog (II)

glue

glue

glue

fold over
& glue

fold over
& glue

Cut along dotted lines

Flower

tab

fold under

Lily Pad

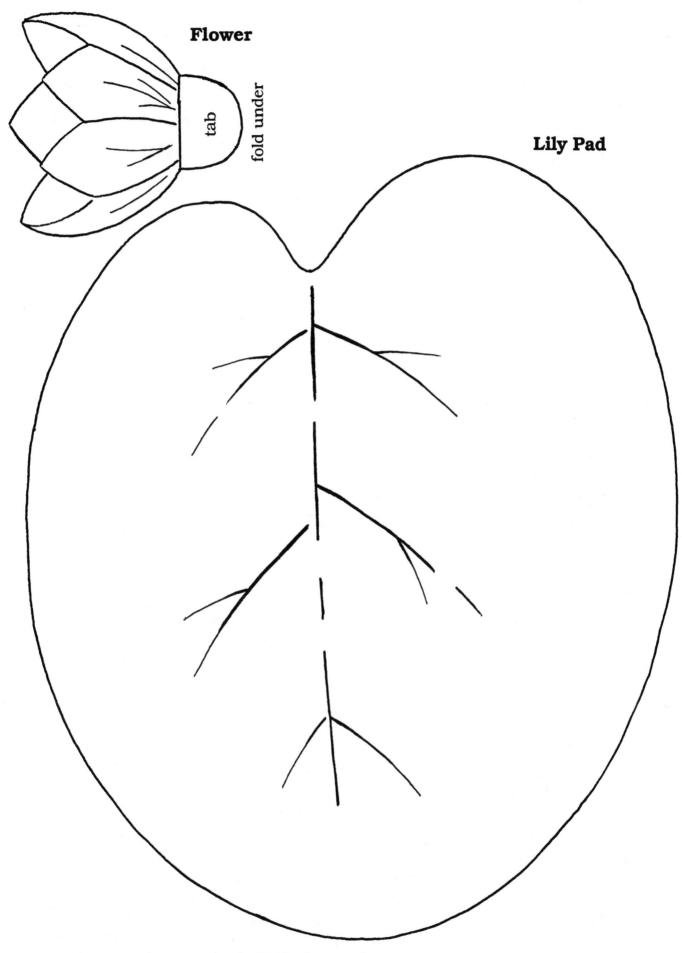

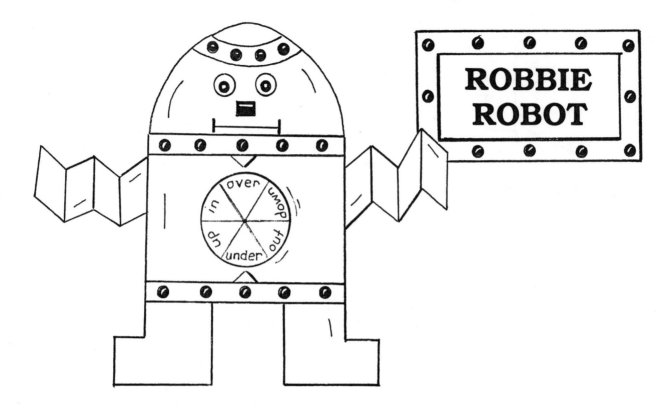

MATERIALS:
- construction paper
- crayons or markers
- glue
- scissors
- brads

CONSTRUCTION:
1. Reproduce and cut out the patterns.
2. Cut the patterns out of construction paper and/or color the patterns with crayons or markers.
3. Fold the robot arms like a fan and glue them to the robot.
4. Write opposites on the wheel (write word pairs across from one another as shown above). Insert a brad through the center of the wheel and attach it to the robot. The "arrows" on the robot point to the opposites.

USE:
- Display the robot on a bulletin board or wall.
  - Make more than one wheel to teach different concepts such as capital and lower-case letters, numerals and number words, synonyms, homonyms, rhyming words, etc.
  - Make several blank wheels and place them near the robot. Have the students supply "information" to reinforce specific topics. (Note: Questions and answers may be written "opposite" each other on the wheel.)

Robot Arm

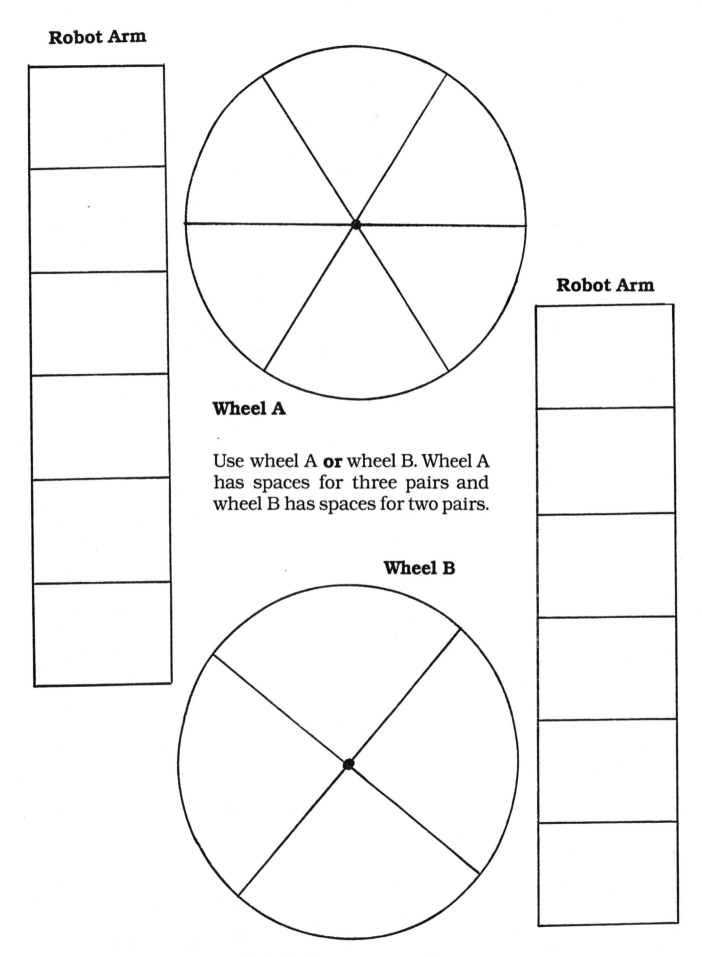

Wheel A

Use wheel A **or** wheel B. Wheel A has spaces for three pairs and wheel B has spaces for two pairs.

Wheel B

Robot Arm

Robot

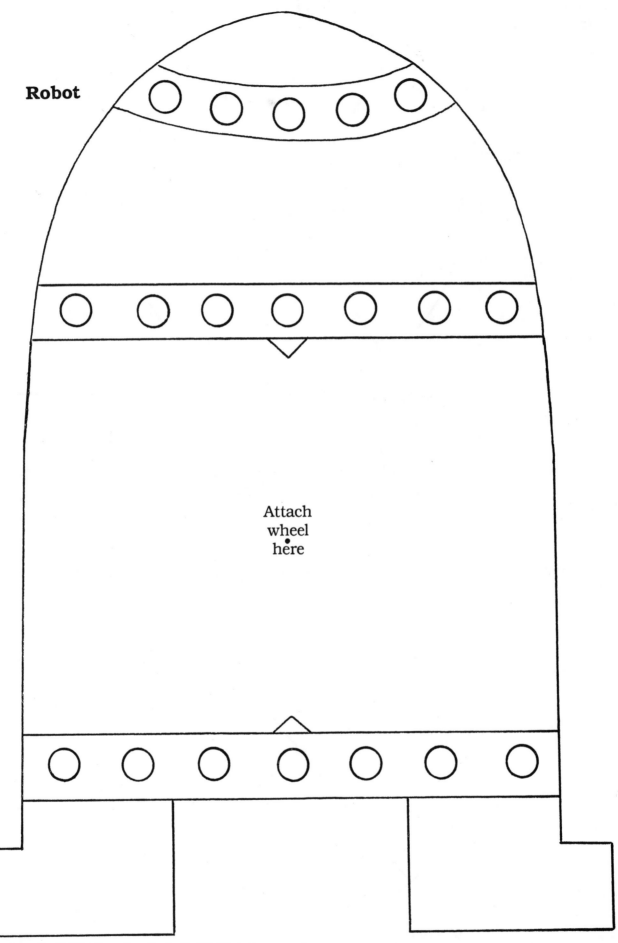

Attach
wheel
•
here

THE LITTLE LEARNING ENGINE

MATERIALS:
- construction paper
- crayons or markers
- glue
- scissors
- brads

CONSTRUCTION:
1. Reproduce and cut out the patterns.
2. Cut the patterns out of construction paper and/or color the patterns with crayons or markers. Draw an engineer in the engineer's seat. (For individual student projects, each student may draw himself or herself in the engineer's seat.)
3. Cut the wheels labeled "A" along the dotted lines. Glue these wheels to the wheels labeled "B."
4. Insert a brad through the center of each wheel and attach the wheels to the engine.

USE:
- Let each student make his or her own engine to use in reviewing skills and concepts. (Write a word or problem on each "flap" and the corresponding words or answers beneath the flaps.)
- Display the engine on a "railroad" bulletin board (railroad tracks, scenery, puffs of smoke for the caption "All Aboard The Little Learning Engine"). Use the engine to teach skills and concepts. When it's time to change skills, just change the wheels!

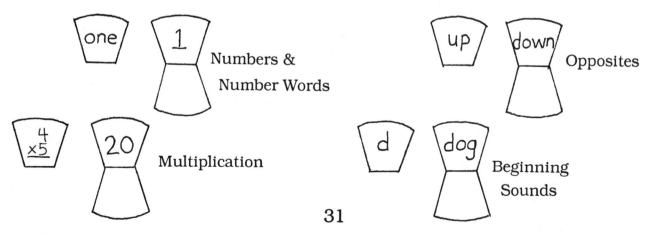

Engine

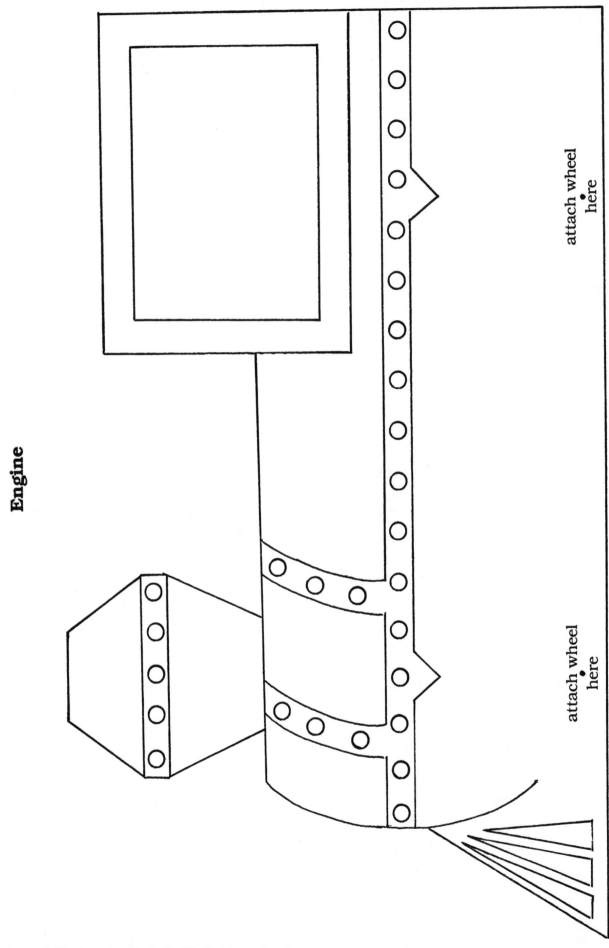

attach wheel here

attach wheel here

brad

glue

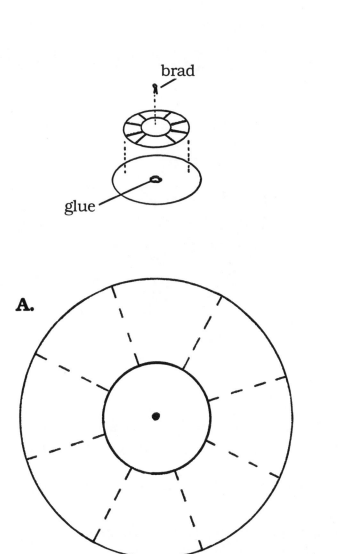

A.

B.

glue
here

cut along dotted lines

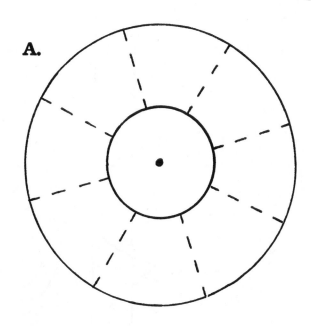

A.

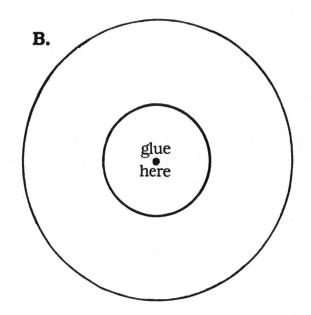

B.

glue
here

BUBBLES THE GOLDFISH

MATERIALS:
- construction paper
- glue
- crayons or markers
- scissors

CONSTRUCTION:
1. Reproduce and cut out the fish and fishbowl patterns.
2. Cut the patterns out of construction paper and/or color them with crayons or markers.
3. Use a black marker to write the alphabet or the numerals 1-26 on the bubbles "inside" the fishbowl.
4. Fold the fishbowl in half and cut along the dotted lines.
5. Fold the tabs on the goldfish and slide them through the slits in the fishbowl. Glue the tabs together.

USE:
- Have the students move Bubbles back and forth across the fishbowl as they recite the alphabet or count aloud.
- Students may work addition, subtraction, multiplication and division problems by moving Bubbles to the appropriate numerals.
- Encourage students to practice spelling vocabulary words by moving Bubbles to the appropriate letters in the correct sequence.

Goldfish

Fishbowl

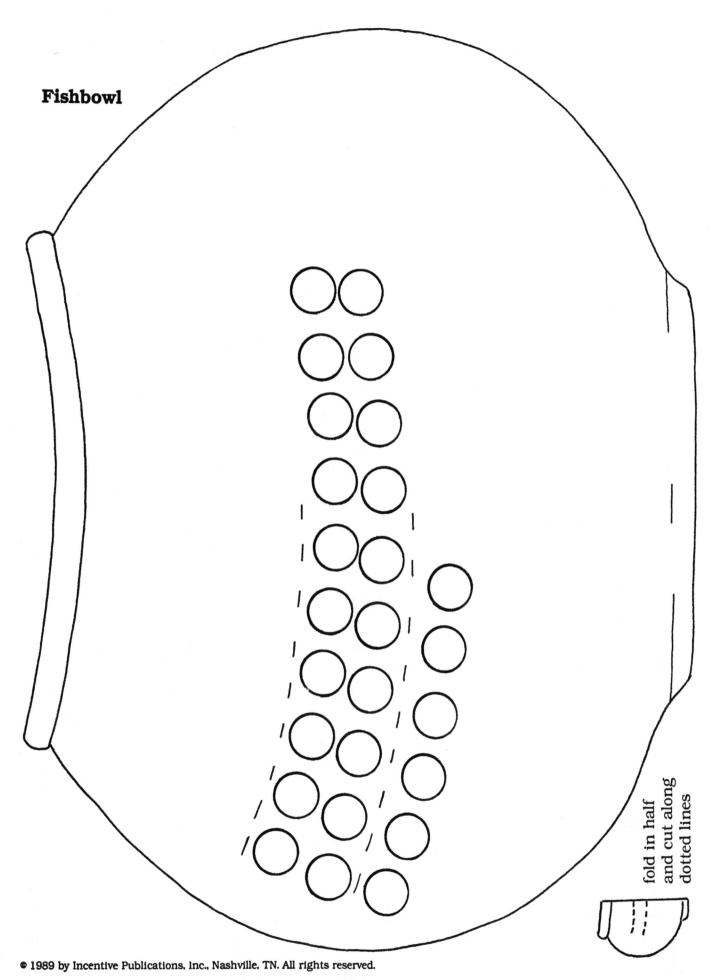

fold in half
and cut along
dotted lines

KATIE THE KANGAROO

MATERIALS:
- construction paper
- crayons or markers
- scissors
- glue
- paper lunch sacks

CONSTRUCTION:
1. Reproduce and cut out the patterns.
2. Cut the patterns out of construction paper and/or color the patterns with crayons or markers.
3. Cut the top off of the sack four inches from the bottom.
4. Glue the kangaroo's upper body to the sack so that the arms hang down inside the sack.
5. Glue the legs to each side of the sack and the tail to the back of the sack.

USE:
- Each student can write his or her name on a kangaroo (on the front of the sack) and use the kangaroo to hold crayons, pencils, scissors, glue, or other items.
- Make several kangaroos to use for bulletin board games. Attach a large sack to the board. Make flashcards to be placed in the large sack. Instruct the students to match the flashcards with the corresponding kangaroos (see below).

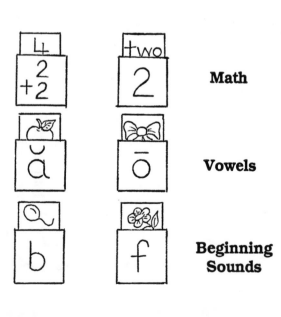

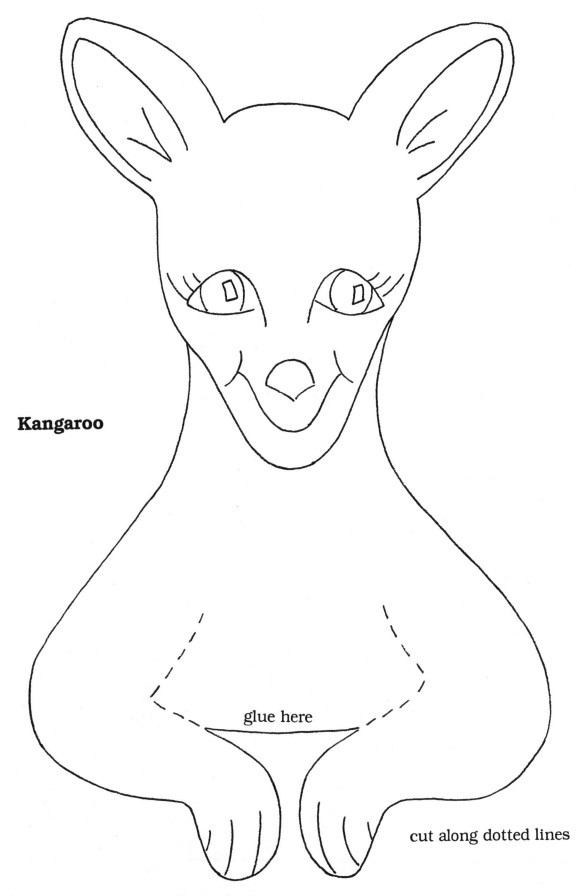

Kangaroo

glue here

cut along dotted lines

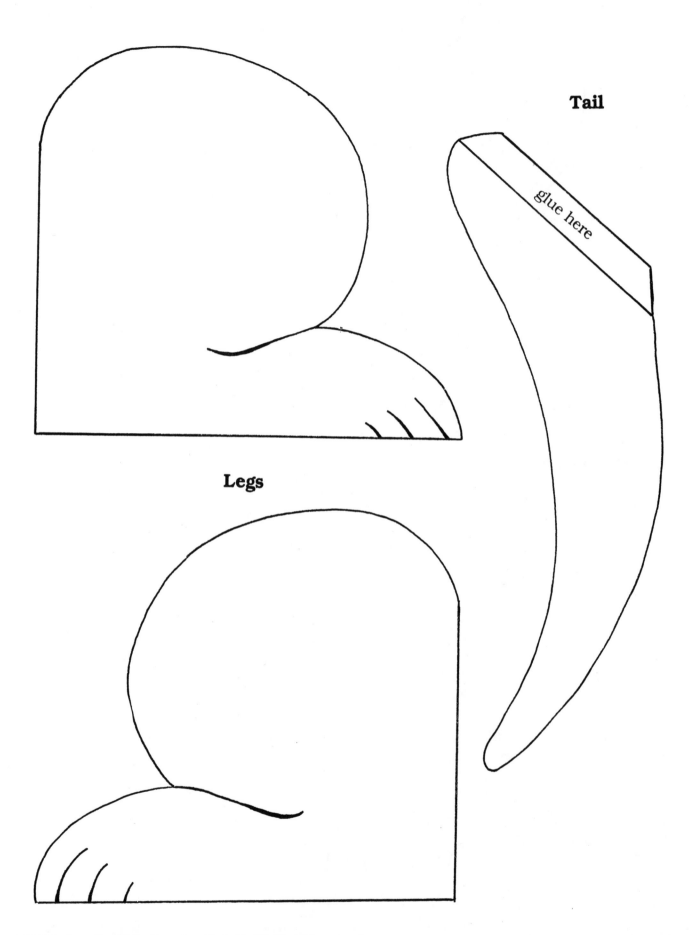

Tail

glue here

Legs

TURTLE TOWN

MATERIALS:
- construction paper
- crayons or markers
- glue
- scissors

CONSTRUCTION:
1. Reproduce and cut out the patterns.
2. Cut the patterns out of construction paper and/or color the patterns with crayons or markers.
3. Glue each pair of vowel pictures on a colorful sheet of construction paper.
4. Cut a "post" out of brown construction paper for each vowel sheet. Glue the mounted vowel pictures to the posts.
5. Construct the turtle as instructed on the pattern page.

USE:
- Create a bulletin board display to teach long and short vowel sounds. Attach the vowel signs and a sign that reads "Come To Turtle Town To Learn The Vowel Sounds" to the board. Each student can make a 3-D turtle for the board.
- Use the vowel pictures as flashcards or as patterns for name tags, bulletin board decorations, etc.

Turtle

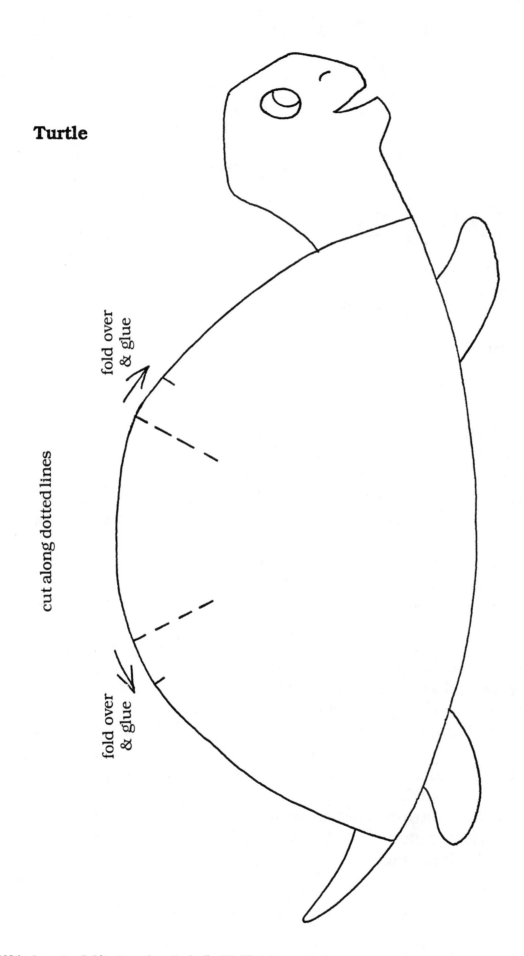

cut along dotted lines

fold over & glue

fold over & glue

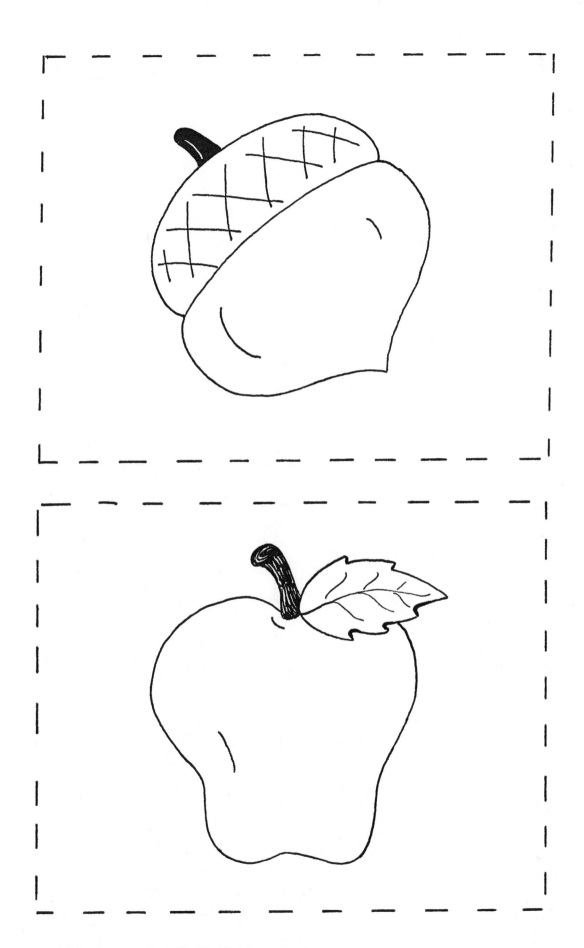

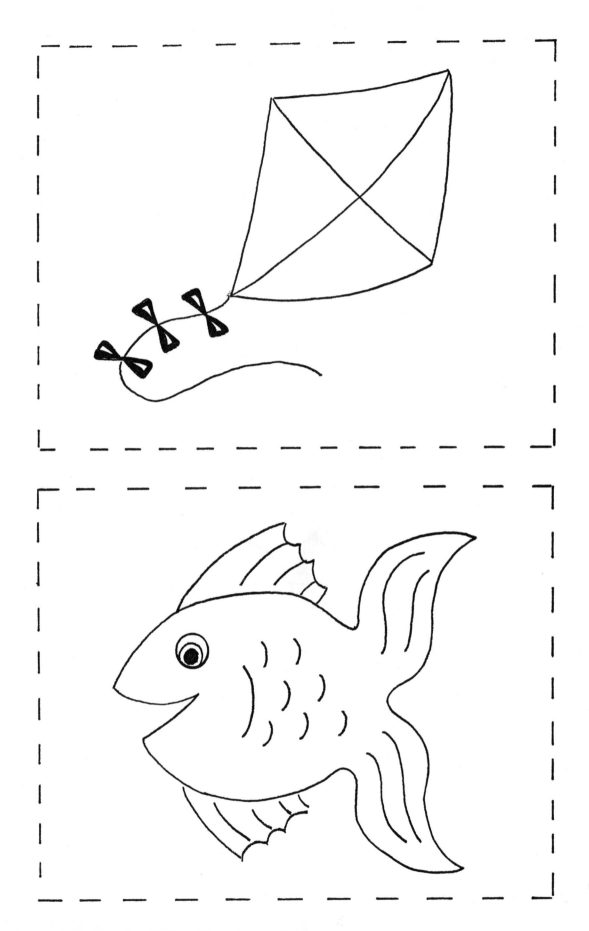

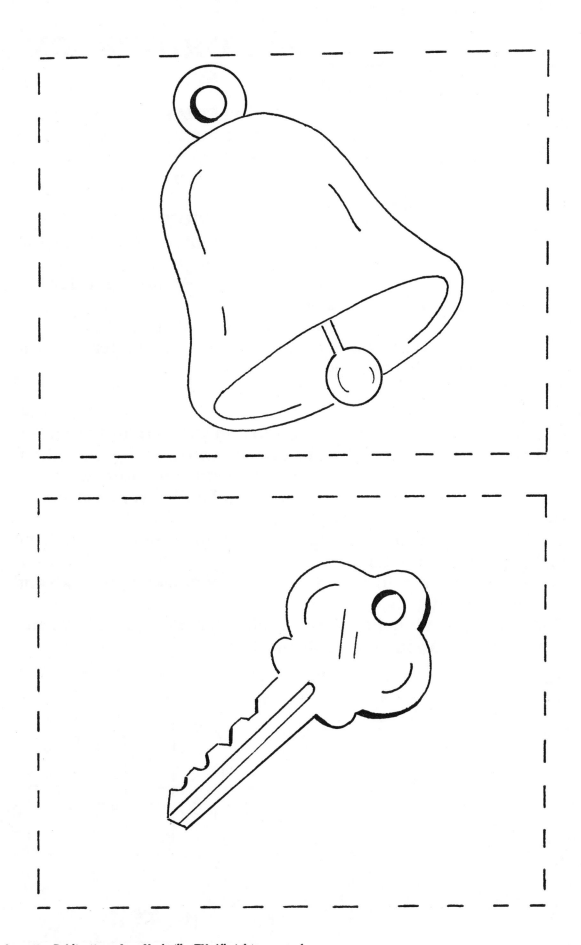

WORDY WORM

MATERIALS:
- construction paper
- crayons or markers
- scissors

CONSTRUCTION:
1. Reproduce and cut out the pattern.
2. Cut the pattern out of construction paper and/or color the pattern with crayons or markers.
3. Construct the worm as instructed on the pattern page.
4. Write "information" on and under the tabs to teach basic concepts and skills as suggested below.

USE:
- Have each student construct a worm and write "information" on and under the tabs such as beginning consonant blends, final consonant blends, rhyming words, numerals and number words, math problems, color recognition, capital and lower-case letters, etc.
- Students can make greeting cards or invitations by writing messages under the tabs!
- Make question and answer games. Write a question on a tab and the answer under the tab.
- Encourage the students to think of other uses for the worms. Display the creations on a bulletin board.

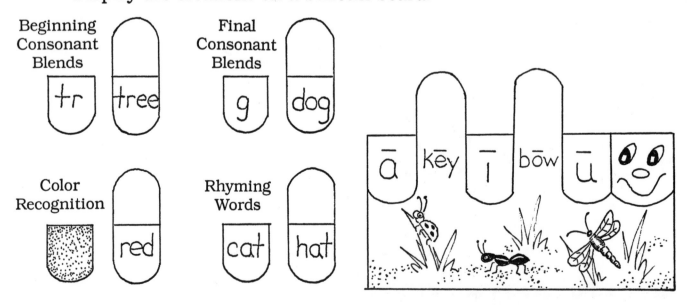

Beginning Consonant Blends — tr tree

Final Consonant Blends — g dog

Color Recognition — red

Rhyming Words — cat hat

Worm

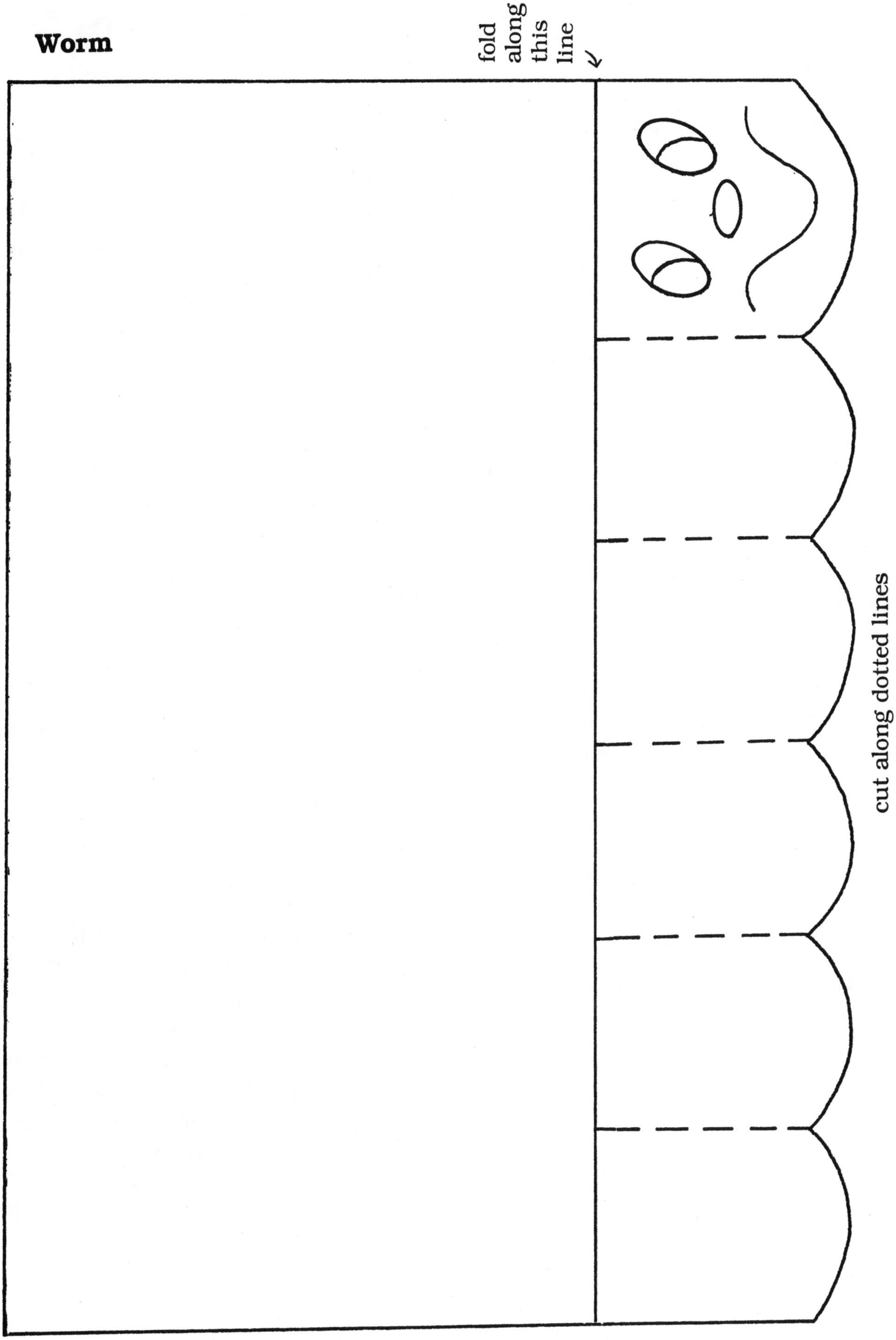

cut along dotted lines

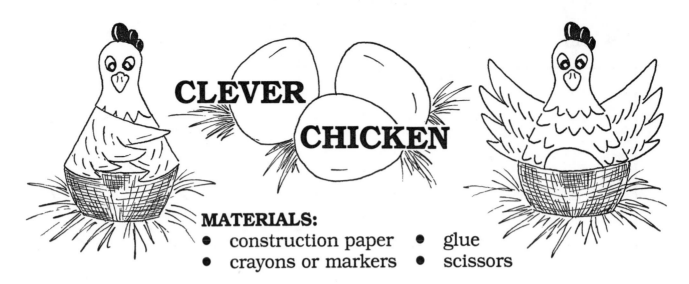

CLEVER CHICKEN

MATERIALS:
- construction paper
- crayons or markers
- glue
- scissors

CONSTRUCTION:
1. Reproduce and cut out the patterns.
2. Cut the patterns out of construction paper and/or color the patterns with crayons or markers.
3. Apply a thin line of glue around the outer sides of the nest. Fold the nest **up** along the dotted lines.
4. Fold the chicken's wings along the dotted lines.
5. Write "information" on the eggs and place the eggs in the nest.

USE:
- Use the eggs as flashcards for practicing basic skills (see examples below). Store the eggs in the nest.
- Write special treats and privileges on eggs and place the eggs in the chicken's nest. Display the chicken on a bulletin board with the caption "Be A Good Egg To Hatch A Special Treat!" List the ways students may earn treats on the board. When a student qualifies, let him or her draw an egg from the nest and enjoy a special treat!
- Write topics for stories or art projects on eggs and place the eggs in the nest. Display the chicken on a bulletin board. Let each student draw an egg and complete a project for that topic. Display the completed projects on the bulletin board.

Egg

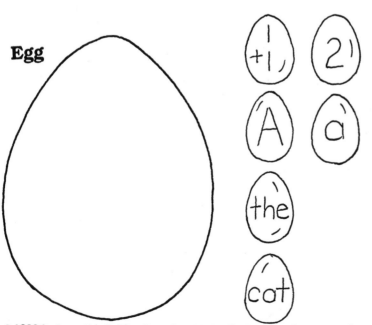

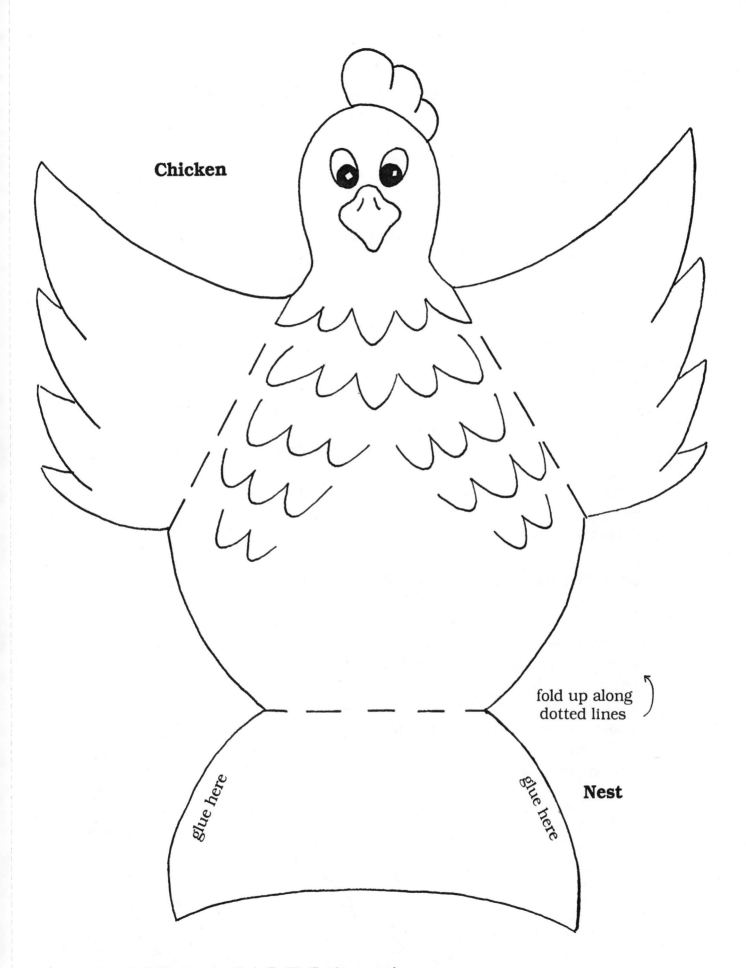

Chicken

fold up along
dotted lines

glue here

glue here

Nest

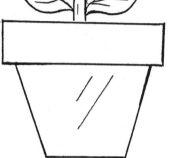

FROM SEED TO PLANT

MATERIALS:
- construction paper
- crayons or markers
- glue
- scissors

CONSTRUCTION:
1. Reproduce and cut out the patterns.
2. Cut the patterns out of construction paper and/or color the patterns with crayons or markers.
3. Glue the center of the flower to the petals. Glue the flower to the stem.
4. Fold the flowerpot in half and glue the flower stem to the back of the pot.
5. Glue the seed to the root and glue this to the inside of the flowerpot.
6. Label the parts of the seed and the plant.

USE:
- Let each student assemble a flower and flowerpot to become familiar with the structure of a plant.
- Make greeting cards or invitations. Write messages inside the flowerpots (omit the seed structure).
- Display the flowers on a springtime bulletin board.

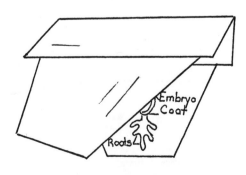

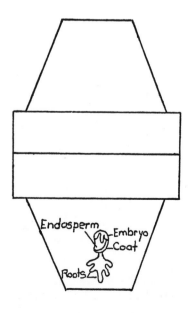

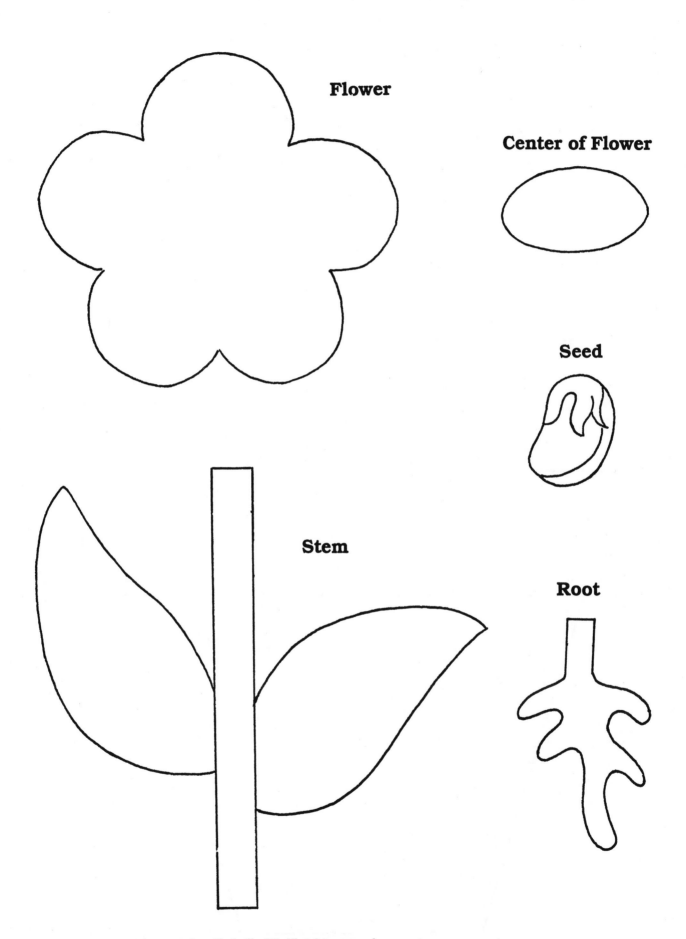

Flower

Center of Flower

Seed

Stem

Root

Flowerpot

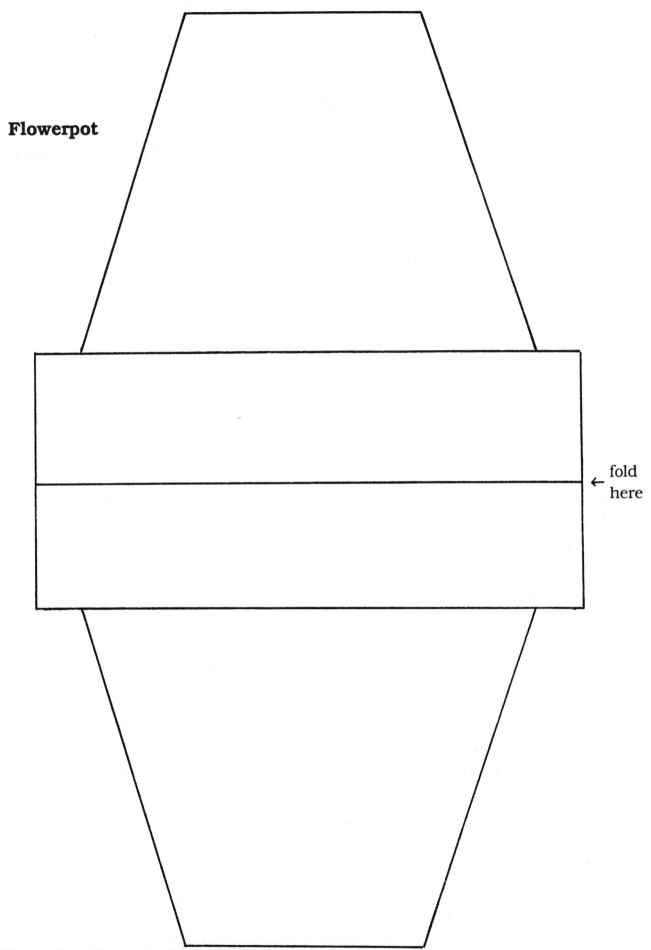

fold
here

I WONDER WHAT'S UNDER THE SEA

MATERIALS:
- construction paper
- crayons or markers
- glue
- scissors

CONSTRUCTION:
1. Reproduce and cut out the patterns.
2. Cut the patterns out of construction paper and/or color the patterns with crayons or markers.
3. Glue the sail to the boat.
4. Draw sea creatures on the ocean pattern.
5. Follow the instructions on the pattern page to attach the boat to the ocean.

USE:
- Students will enjoy making movable boats when they are studying the sea and sea life. Display the boats on a bulletin board.
- Have each student write a simple poem about the sea on the ocean pattern. Display the 3-D poem projects for all to enjoy.

Sail

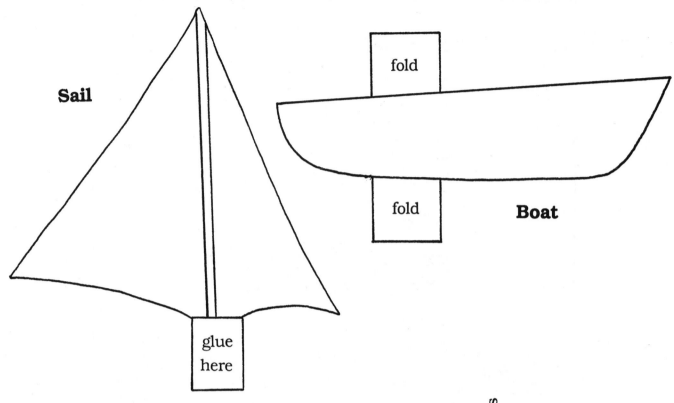

Boat

fold

fold

glue
here

To Attach Boat To Ocean:

1. Fold the ocean pattern in half and cut along the dotted lines.
2. Fold back the tabs on the boat.
3. Slide the tabs through the slits in the ocean pattern and glue the tabs together.

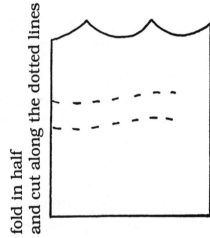

fold in half
and cut along the dotted lines

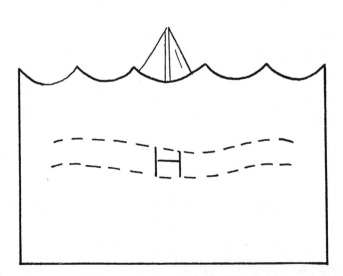

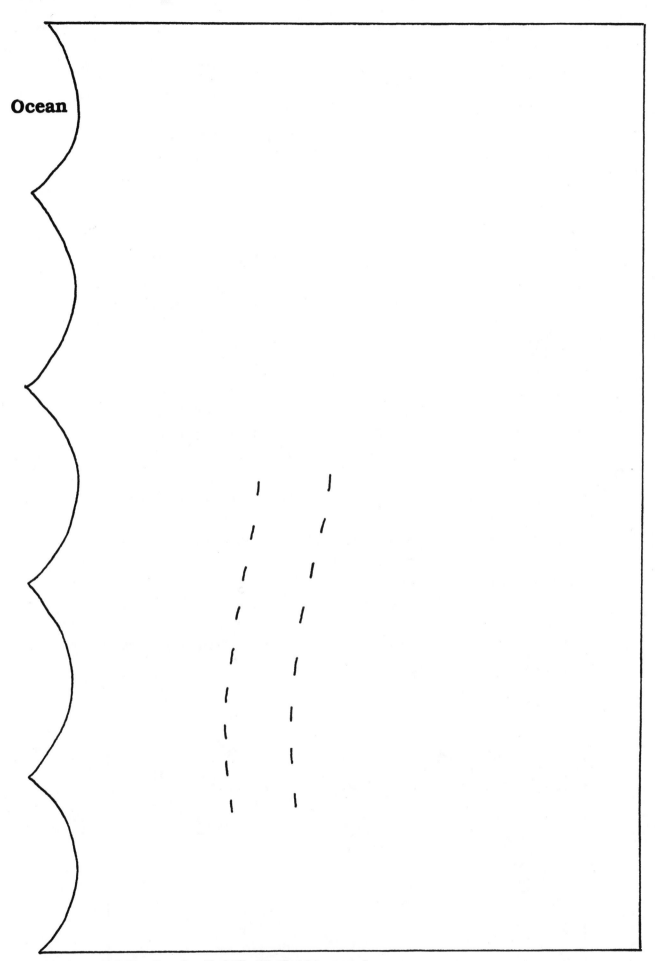

Ocean

fold in half & cut along dotted lines

DINOSAURS

MATERIALS:
- construction paper
- crayons or markers
- glue
- scissors

CONSTRUCTION:
1. Reproduce and cut out the patterns.
2. Cut the patterns out of construction paper and/or color the patterns with crayons or markers.
3. Construct the dinosaurs as instructed on the pattern pages.

USE:
- Create a "prehistoric" bulletin board on which to display Triceratops and Stegosaurus.
- Construct a 3-D dinosaur scene. Place a table against a wall and cover the table with green construction paper. Draw a prehistoric setting on butcher paper and attach it to the wall behind the table. Let each student make a dinosaur to place in the scene. (Tape Triceratops and Stegosaurus to the wall. Place Tyrannosaurus and Brontosaurus on the table.) Add a construction paper pond and other scenery if desired.

Triceratops

fold over & glue

cut along dotted lines

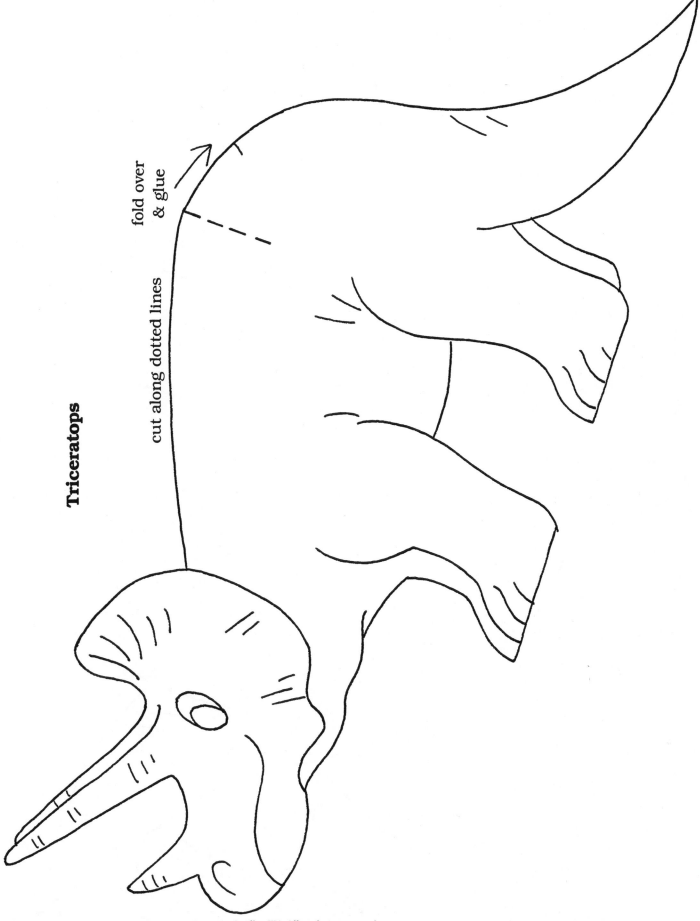

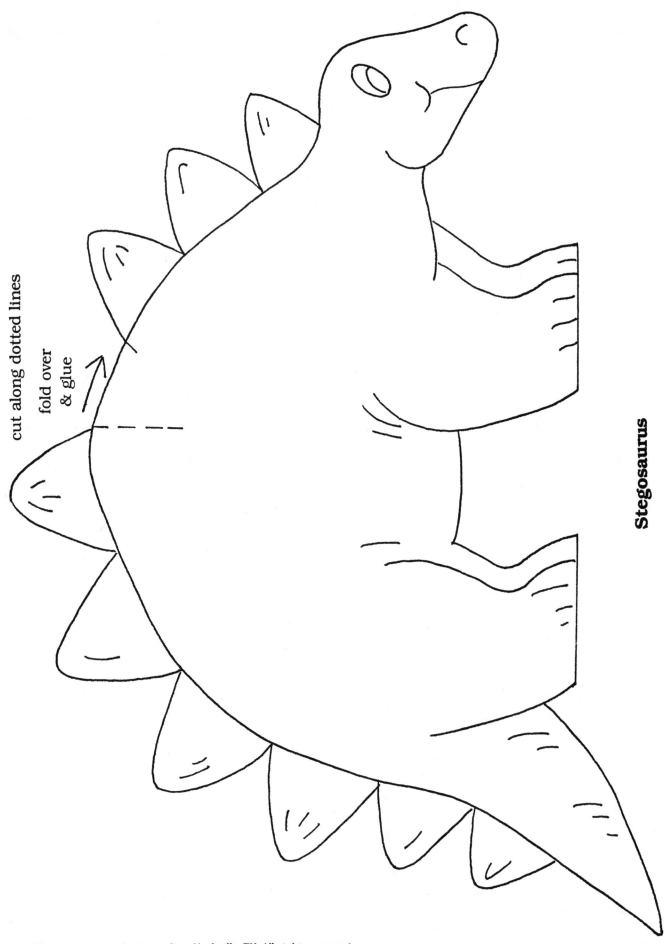

cut along dotted lines

fold over & glue

Stegosaurus

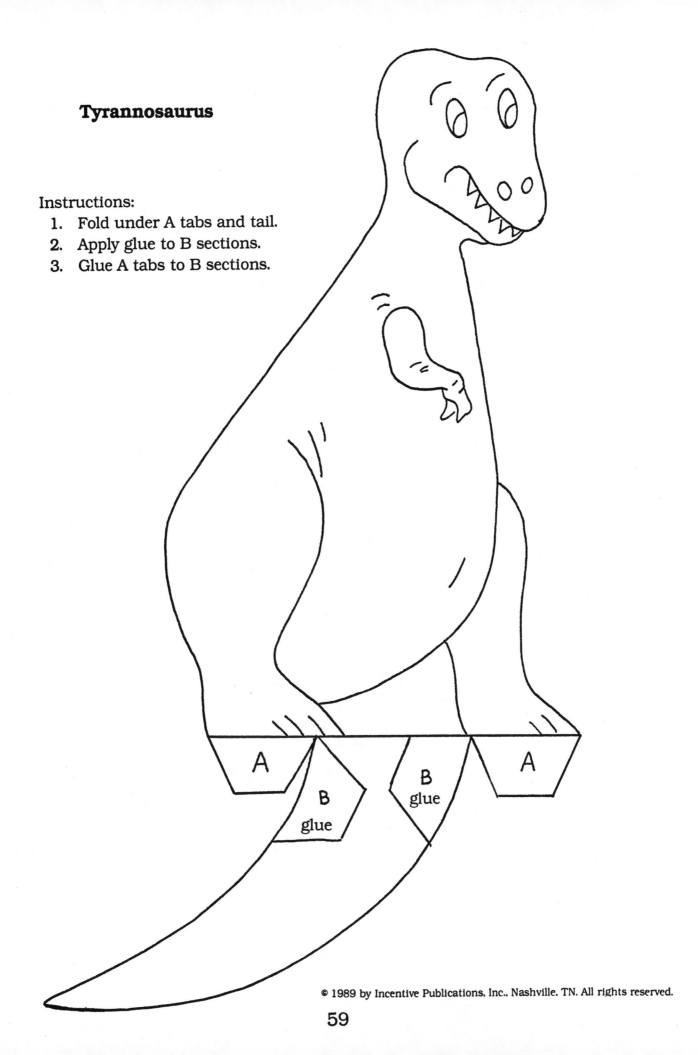

Tyrannosaurus

Instructions:
1. Fold under A tabs and tail.
2. Apply glue to B sections.
3. Glue A tabs to B sections.

A

B
glue

B
glue

A

Brontosaurus

Instructions:
1. Fold under A tabs and tail.
2. Apply glue to B sections.
3. Glue A tabs to B sections.

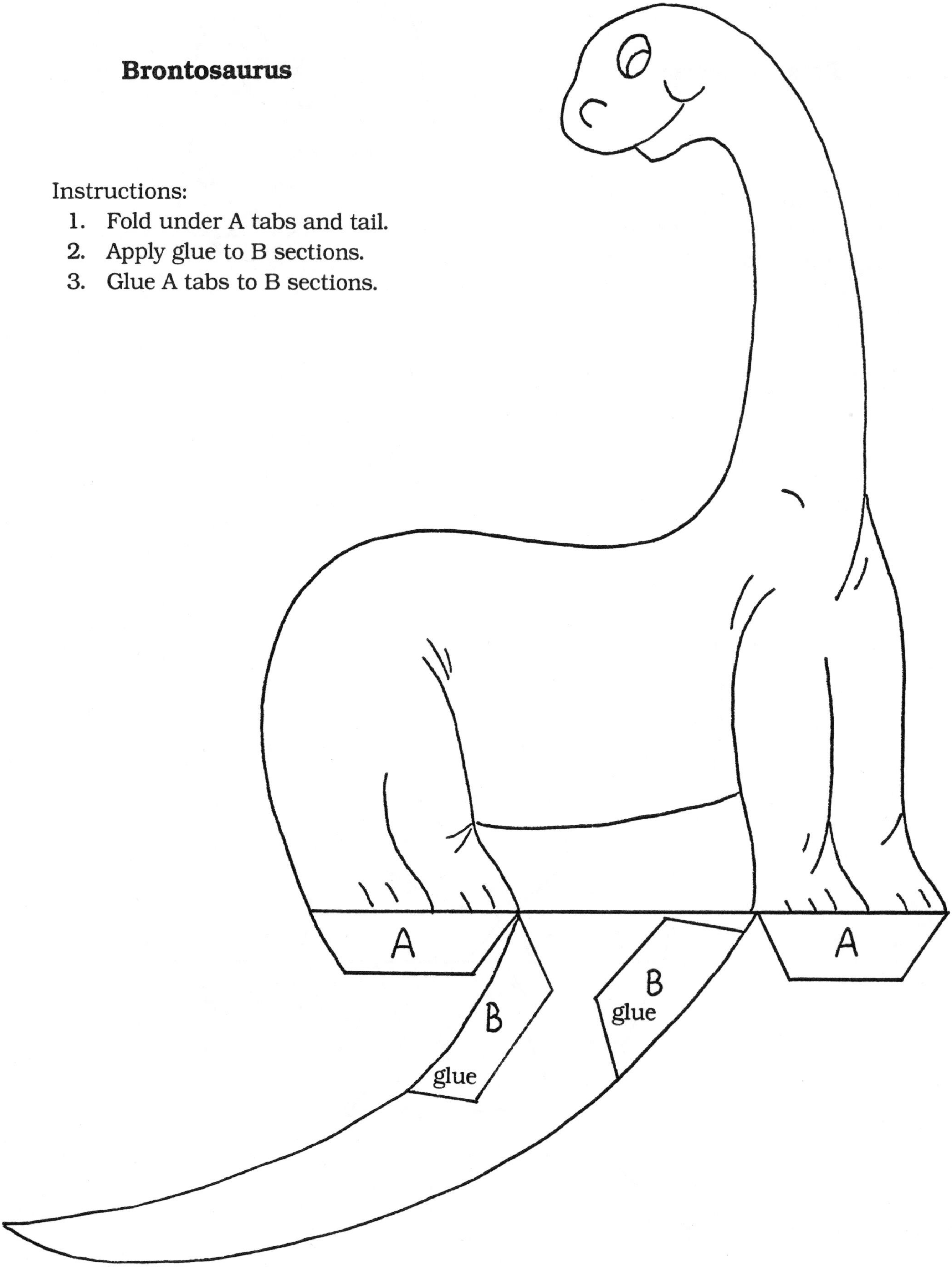

A

A

B

glue

B

glue

PAPER PALS

A Paper Pal For The Holidays

MATERIALS:
- construction paper
- crayons or markers
- scissors
- glue

CONSTRUCTION:
1. Reproduce and cut out the patterns.
2. Cut the patterns out of construction paper and/or color them with crayons or markers.

   Note: To cut the paper pals' mouths, fold the patterns in half and cut along the dotted lines.

BOO!

A Halloween Paper Pal For Scary Ghost Stories And Spooky Artwork.

USE:
- Paper pals are a fun way to display students' work!
- Write messages on the paper pals and use them as "certificates" to motivate students to do good work.

Dog

cut along
dotted lines

Cat

Ghost

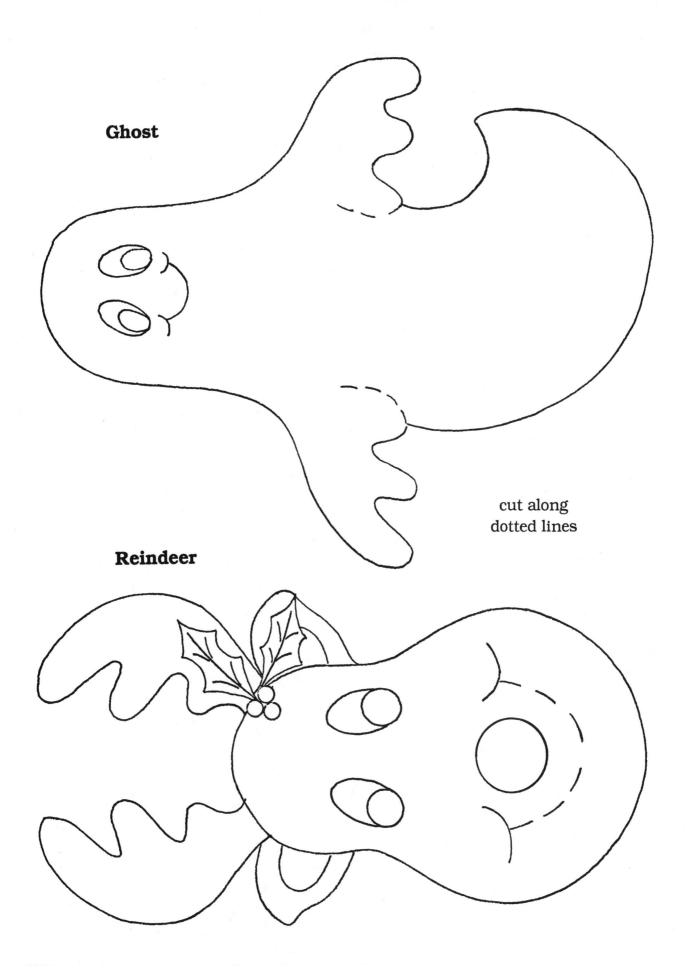

cut along
dotted lines

Reindeer

Bear

Bunny

cut along
dotted lines

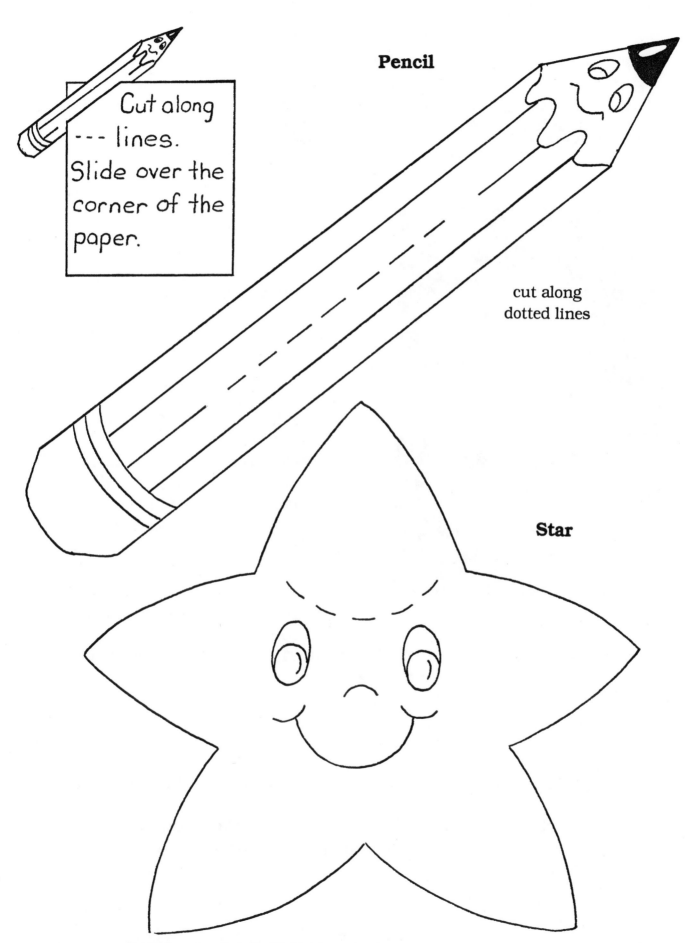

Pencil

Cut along
--- lines.
Slide over the
corner of the
paper.

cut along
dotted lines

Star

POP-UP GHOST

MATERIALS:
- construction paper
- crayons or markers
- glue
- scissors

CONSTRUCTION:
1. Reproduce and cut out the patterns.
2. Cut the patterns out of construction paper and/or color the patterns with crayons or markers. Draw a face on the pumpkin to make a jack-o'-lantern.
3. Cut off the top of the pumpkin and glue it to the top of the ghost.
4. Glue the **outer** edges of the pumpkin to a sheet of black construction paper (do not glue the top).
5. Slide the ghost into the pumpkin. Pull the stem to make the ghost pop up!

USE:
- Every student will enjoy making a pop-up ghost as a Halloween art project.
- Make party invitations! Write the party information on the ghost.
- Write Halloween jokes or riddles on the pumpkins and the answers on the ghosts.

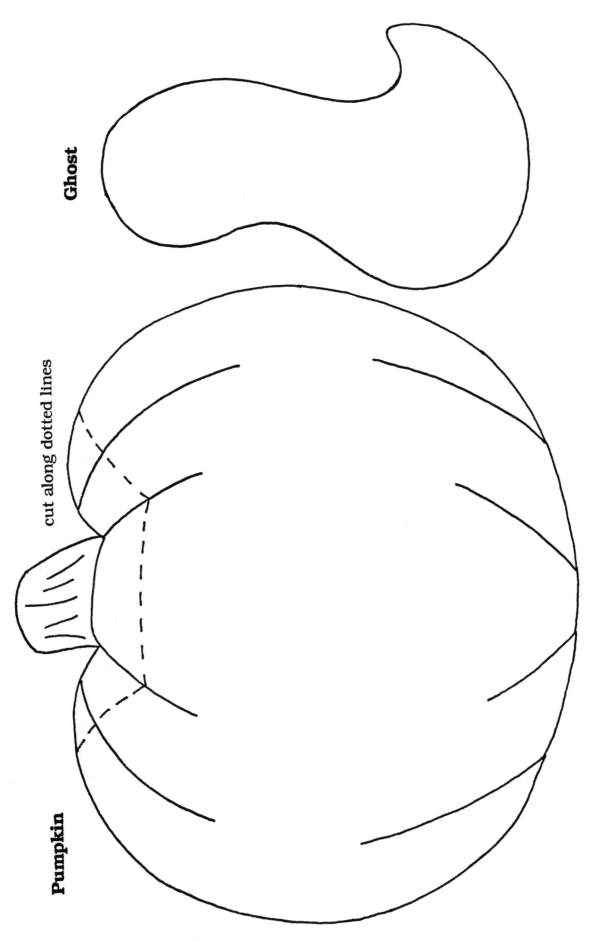

Ghost

cut along dotted lines

Pumpkin

TERRIFIC TURKEY

MATERIALS:
- construction paper
- crayons or markers
- glue
- scissors
- leaves and typing paper (optional)

CONSTRUCTION:
1. Reproduce and cut out the patterns.
2. Cut the patterns out of construction paper and/or color the patterns with crayons or markers.
3. Cut, fold and glue the turkey as instructed on the pattern page.
4. Glue the tail feathers to the back of the turkey.

   Option: Make leaf rubbings for the tail feathers. Place a small leaf beneath a sheet of typing paper and rub over the leaf with a crayon. (Always rub in the same direction.)

USE:
- Write "information" on the tail feathers (such as numerals) to reinforce skills or concepts.
- Have the students make leaf rubbings as instructed above. Cut out the rubbings and glue them to the turkeys for tail feathers. Mount the turkeys on construction paper backgrounds or display them on a bulletin board.

Turkey　　　　**Tail Feather**

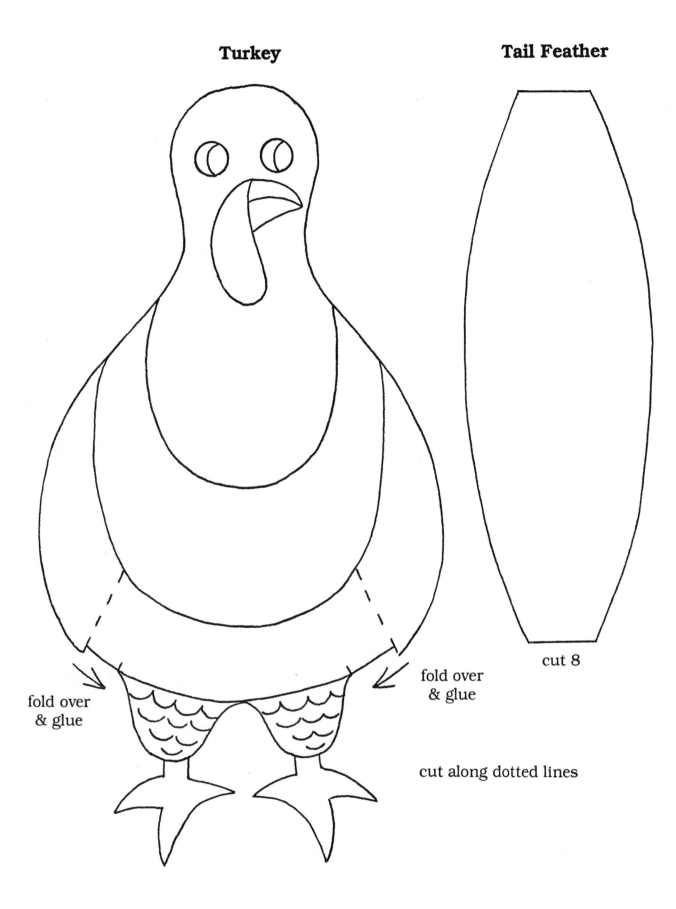

cut 8

fold over
& glue

fold over
& glue

cut along dotted lines

LOLLIPOP ORNAMENTS

MATERIALS:
- lightweight cardboard
- wooden craft sticks
- scissors
- glue
- crayons or markers
- silver glitter
- hole punch
- yarn or ribbon
- wrapping paper (seasonal)
- ornament hooks

CONSTRUCTION:
1. Reproduce and cut out the pattern.
2. Trace around the pattern on lightweight cardboard. Cut out two circles for each lollipop.
3. Draw a picture on each circle pattern with crayons or markers, or cut designs out of seasonal wrapping paper to glue on the circles.
4. Spread a thin layer of glue over the circles and sprinkle silver glitter over the glue.
5. Glue a wooden craft stick between two circles to make a lollipop.
6. Punch a hole in the top of the lollipop and insert an ornament hook. Tie a ribbon or piece of yarn around the lollipop.

USE:
- Students will enjoy making lollipop ornaments to decorate the classroom or to take home! (Lollipop ornaments make great gifts!)

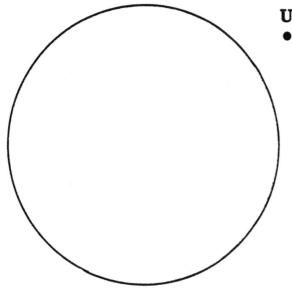

Lollipop

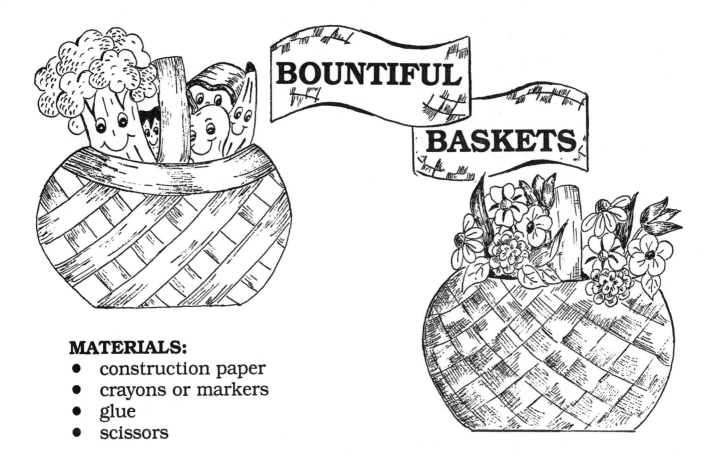

BOUNTIFUL BASKETS

MATERIALS:
- construction paper
- crayons or markers
- glue
- scissors

CONSTRUCTION:
1. Reproduce and cut out the patterns.
2. Cut the patterns out of construction paper and/or color the patterns with crayons or markers. (Draw funny faces on the food if you like.)
3. Apply glue to the outer edges of the basket (do not glue the top). Fold the basket in half and press it together.
4. Apply glue to each side of the handle and attach it to the basket.
5. Fill the basket with flowers or fruit.

USE:
- Display a basket filled with food from the four food groups to encourage good eating habits. Create a bulletin board display which gives information about the four food groups.
- Have each student make a basket and a "set" of food items. Instruct the students to write their names on their baskets. Display the baskets on a bulletin board or wall. Each day, have each student place a representative food in his or her basket for every food group he or she ate the day before. (This will encourage students to take notice of what they eat!)
- Students may fill their baskets with flowers and display them on a wall, door or bulletin board to decorate the room with springtime colors. (Spring baskets make great Mother's Day gifts!)

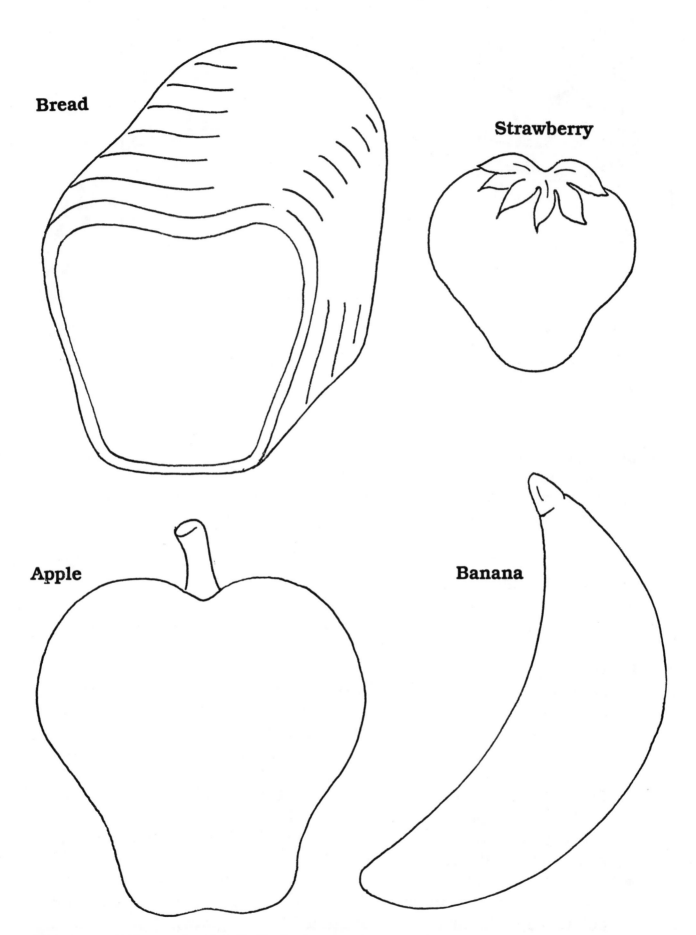

Bread

Strawberry

Apple

Banana

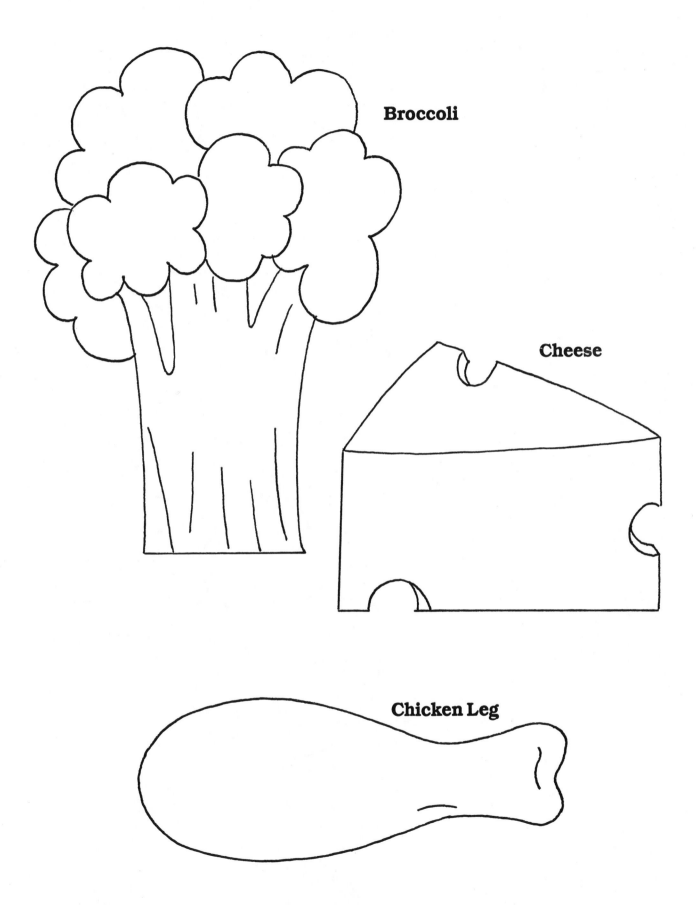

Broccoli

Cheese

Chicken Leg

Flowers

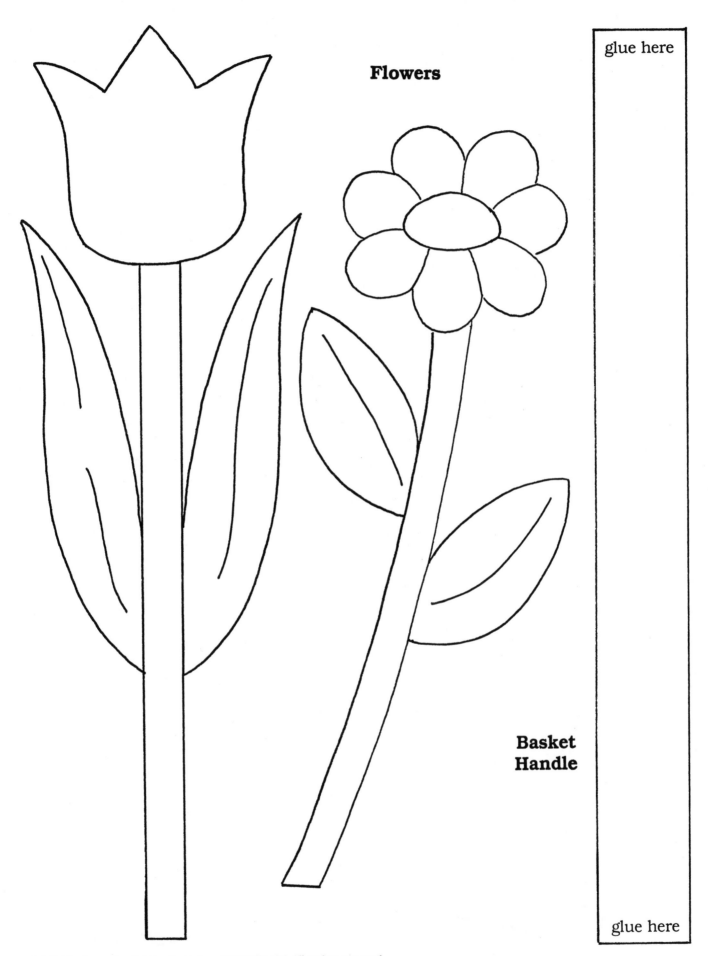

Flowers

glue here

**Basket
Handle**

glue here

75

Basket

fold here →

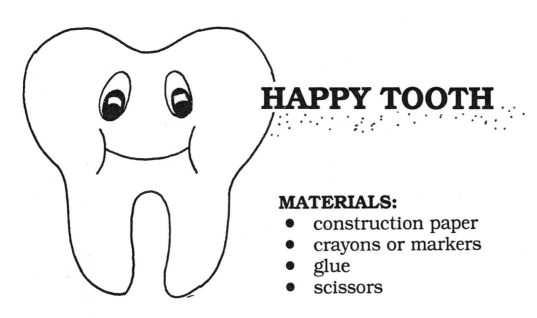

HAPPY TOOTH

MATERIALS:
- construction paper
- crayons or markers
- glue
- scissors

CONSTRUCTION:
1. Reproduce and cut out the patterns.
2. Cut the patterns out of construction paper and/or color the patterns with crayons or markers.
3. Cut a long "strip" of white paper for the toothpaste and glue it to the toothpaste tube.
4. Construct a 3-D tooth as instructed on the pattern page.

USE:
- Create a bulletin board display. Write this message on the toothpaste strip: "Brush Your Teeth Every Day To Help Stop Tooth Decay." Let each student make a 3-D tooth for the board.
- Have each student make a 3-D tooth and glue it to a sheet of construction paper. Each student may write good dental habits beneath his or her "happy" tooth.

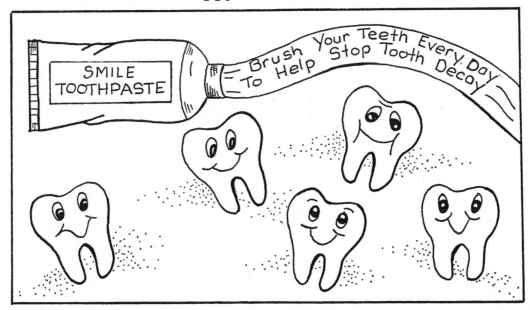

Tooth

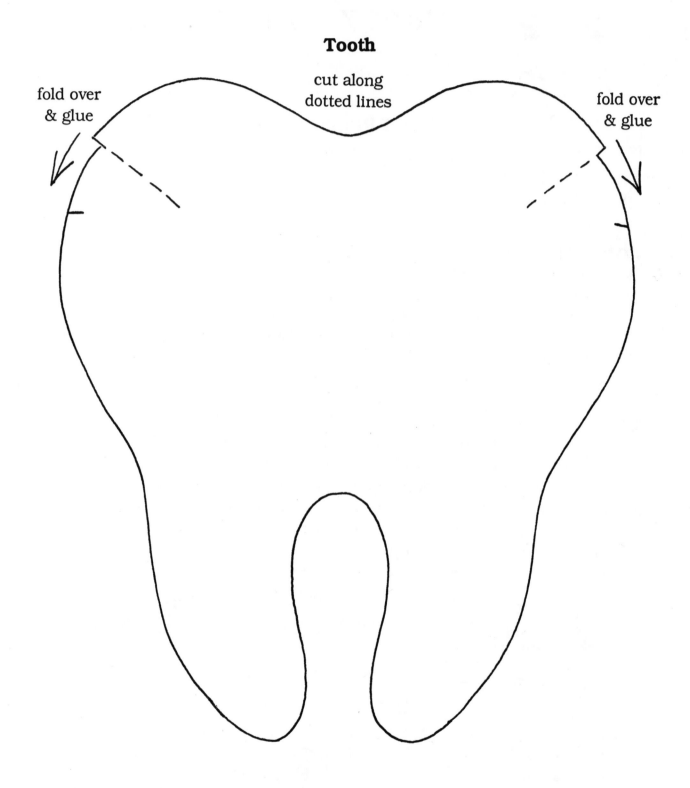

fold over & glue

cut along dotted lines

fold over & glue

Toothpaste Tube

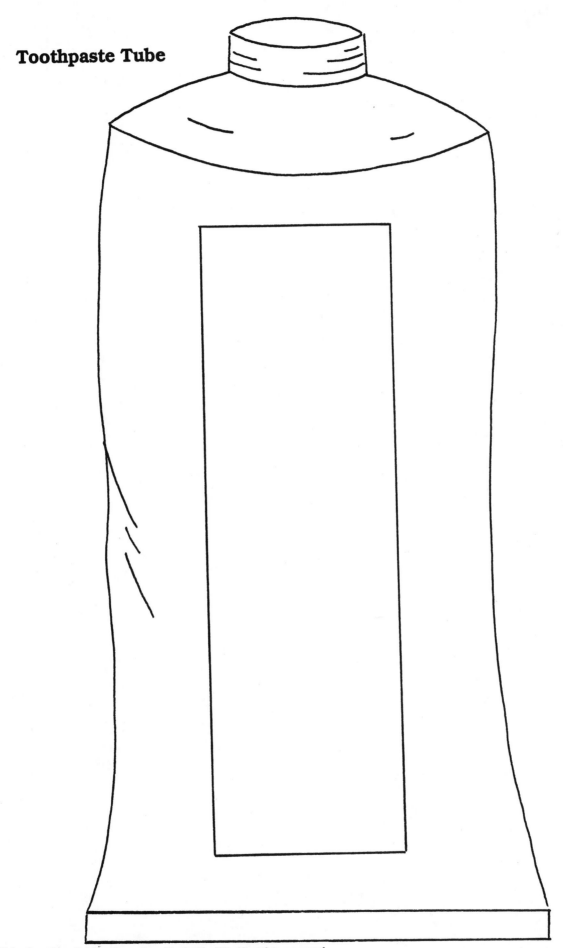